IMAGES
of America

DOVER

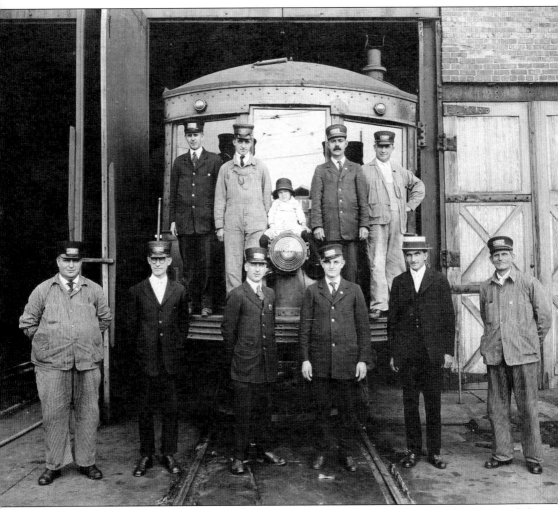

Employees of the Northern Ohio Traction and Light Company are pictured in front of the Wooster Avenue streetcar barn around 1921. From left to right are (first row) Herbert Patton, Roy Cox, Harrison Wolf, Orrin Mohn, Herbert Hamilton, and Joe McCartney; (second row) Edward Peacock, Bill Seggett, unidentified, William Bayless, and W. E. Zimmerman. (Courtesy of the Dover Historical Society.)

On the cover: See above. (Courtesy of the Dover Historical Society.)

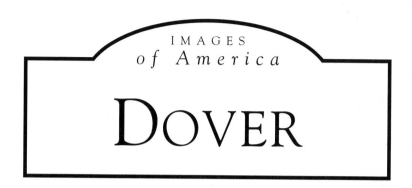

IMAGES
of America

DOVER

Matthew S. Lautzenheiser
on behalf of the Dover Historical Society

ARCADIA
PUBLISHING

Published by Arcadia Publishing
Charleston SC, Chicago IL, Portsmouth NH, San Francisco CA

Printed in the United States of America

Library of Congress Control Number: 2009926229

For all general information contact Arcadia Publishing at:
Telephone 843-853-2070
Fax 843-853-0044
E-mail sales@arcadiapublishing.com
For customer service and orders:
Toll-Free 1-888-313-2665

Visit us on the Internet at www.arcadiapublishing.com

For my father, who taught me to be proud of where I came from.

CONTENTS

ACKNOWLEDGMENTS

As with any project of this scope, there are many people who have helped along the way. Thanks to Arcadia Publishing and my editor, Melissa Basilone, for the opportunity to do a book like this. The work that Arcadia has done over the years to help small historical societies is commendable. There are many historic images that would never have seen the light of day if it were not for the Images of America series. Unless otherwise noted, the images seen here are courtesy of the Dover Historical Society. There were two other entities that contributed images as well. First is the City of Dover, especially Larry Lautzenheiser, superintendent of the Electric Field Division, and Russ Volkert, fire chief. In addition to the information and photographs Volkert provided, he has worked tirelessly to research and document the history of Dover's past. The second outside source of information and photographs was the Tuscarawas County Historical Society. Director Fred Miller and volunteer Tom Yager run a first-class archive and contribute greatly to the preservation of Tuscarawas County's history. With my own organization, the Dover Historical Society, it all begins and ends with the board of trustees. The board approved this project and has been supportive throughout. Board member Bob Liberatore has gone above and beyond the call of duty with his assistance. He filtered through two early drafts of the text and provided keen insights that greatly shaped the final product. In addition to Liberatore, Dover Historical Society curator Kim Jurkovic and past codirectors Jim and Cris Nixon read through early drafts and helped with useful feedback. Also at the Dover Historical Society is longtime volunteer Ruth Richard. She has been involved with the museum for many years and has helped to document and shape the wonderful collection of photographs that make up the majority of this book. Last but certainly not least, I would like to thank my supportive and loving family. My wife, Kelly, and sons, Douglas and Benjamin, are more than I deserve and everything I could ever hope for.

INTRODUCTION

Dover chronicles the town's history in pictures, with images from the 1930s and earlier. While no book can ever be complete or all encompassing, a local history like this is limited by the availability of photographs, information, and space.

The story of a town is not one of inanimate objects or random places but a story of the people who call a place home. While the pictures that follow may feature trains, floods, businesses, and events, the real flesh and bone behind these things are the colorful people who bring them to life. While examining these images of the past, take a moment to reflect on those who toiled away behind the scenes, outside the view of the camera. After all, they are the real Dover.

Dover was founded in 1807 when Pennsylvania natives Christian Deardorff and his brother-in-law Jesse Slingluff purchased land along the Tuscarawas River. When Deardorff built his first bachelor cabin on the banks of the nearby Sugar Creek, there was no town; there was just the vision and potential of the plat map the gentlemen had drawn up. Deardorff's first years in Dover were difficult, living in a one-room cabin and spending his days toiling away building Dover's first flouring mill. The hard work paid off, as Deardorff prospered and built Dover's first store, built the first bridge to cross the Tuscarawas River, became the first postmaster, and served in the Ohio state legislature. His greatest gift to the small village, however, was his influence at the state level in 1825 to secure Dover as a port on the Ohio and Erie Canal. Only nine years after the canal was completed, in 1840, the population of the little village increased tenfold.

The Ohio and Erie Canal was built between 1825 and 1831 and forever changed the fortunes of Dover. When completed, the canal stretched over 300 miles from Cleveland in the north along the shore of Lake Erie to Portsmouth in the south on the banks of the Ohio River. What the canal meant to local farmers was the opportunity to sell their goods and produce to markets all over the United States. Almost overnight, farmers saw the value of their crops nearly triple in price. Milling became big business in Dover, as names like Deardorff, Gintz, and Hardesty capitalized on the available water source and abundance of wheat farms. After the grain was processed, the canal provided a convenient shipping method for the finished product. The Ohio and Erie Canal allowed the bounty of the fertile Tuscarawas River valley to be shipped north and south to national markets.

Building on the prosperity of the canal era, Dover experienced a second boom in the middle of the 19th century with the development of the local blast furnace, the coming of the railroads, and the resulting industry. Creative entrepreneurs and industrialists recognized the assets the Tuscarawas River valley had to offer. Hidden in its rolling hills were the resources necessary to fuel growth. With the blast furnaces and steel mill prospering, mining of both coal and iron ore began in earnest, just as the canal was beginning its steady decline. This growth of industry brought a new wave of people, capital, and innovation to Dover. Industrialist Jeremiah E. Reeves imported Welsh coal miners for their expertise in deep-shaft mining techniques. Along with them also came German and Swiss immigrants looking for opportunity. These newcomers influenced culture, religion, and labor in the valley. As the county industrialized and moved away from an agrarian way of life, men like Reeves ensured a seamless transition. While other towns along the canal struggled as its influence waned, Dover continued to prosper into the 20th century as a result of its transition to industry.

If the canal, industry, and manufacturing can be said to have nurtured Dover's economic growth, then perhaps the individual creativity of its citizens has served to provide its unique character. Many creative and sometimes eccentric individuals have called Dover home at one time or another. From Hollywood actors and playwrights to the world's master carver, Dover has been blessed with many fascinating individuals.

From the time he established his carriage manufactory at Dover in 1868, Samuel J. Toomey strove to produce the highest-quality buggies and carriages available. It was this work ethic and interest in sulky racing that led him to invent the truss axle in the early 1880s. The truss axle revolutionized the sport of sulky racing by producing a stronger yet lighter axle for the one-horse sulkies that were popular during those days. In the 1880s and 1890s, Toomey secured nine patents on his inventions and forever changed the sport he loved.

About the time Toomey was inventing his truss axle, a son was born to struggling Swiss immigrants on October 30, 1885. Ernest "Mooney" Warther's father died when he was only three, and his mother worked tirelessly at washing, mending, and ironing just to keep her family afloat. Young Warther first worked as a herdsman, and later at age 14, he was employed at the American Sheet and Tin Plate Company. It was a chance encounter with a hobo when Warther was working as a cow herder that forever changed his life. The man taught him how to carve a pair of working pliers out of one piece of wood, using only 10 cuts. Warther quickly took to whittling in his spare time and realized he had a natural ability and talent. In 1912, Warther built a workshop and became serious about carving. His dedication paid off, as in 1923, he was offered work with the New York Central Railroad exhibiting his carved trains. He was finally able to quit his job at the steel mill and devote himself to carving full time. Warther spent the years from 1923 until his death in 1973 producing countless works of art, replicating such famous trains as the Great Northern Railway and Pres. Abraham Lincoln's funeral train. He even acquired a bit of fame as a result of his incredible talent, traveling the country exhibiting his carvings and appearing on *The Tonight Show Starring Johnny Carson* in 1965.

Dover native Elliot Nugent carved out his masterpieces with a pen. Nugent was born at 413 Tuscarawas Avenue and attended Dover schools, where he excelled at football and track. Leaving Dover for Ohio State University, Nugent met the man who was to become his greatest collaborator, George Thurber. The two worked on numerous projects together including *The Male Animal*, a Broadway play in which Nugent also starred. During the course of his long career, Nugent was an actor, writer, producer, and director. He authored or coauthored over 20 plays and directed 30 movies.

Men like Toomey, Warther, Nugent, and many others contributed to the creativity and character of the community, reflecting the ideals and work ethic that have come to define the town. It is men like these and thousands of others, forgotten to history, who make the town interesting, successful, and unique.

One

PEOPLE, HOMES, AND HAPPENINGS

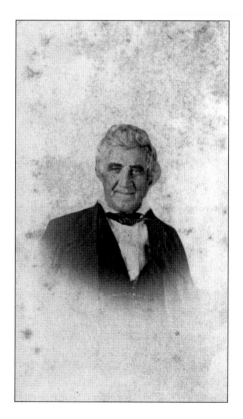

Christian Deardorff was born in York County, Pennsylvania, in 1781 and made his first trip to the Ohio frontier in 1802. Four years later in 1806, he purchased 2,175 acres in what was to become Dover from Col. James Morrison of Lexington, Kentucky. Morrison acquired the land as payment for his service during the Revolutionary War. In 1807, Deardorff moved to Dover, where he spent the next 11 years living in a bachelor's cabin near his water-powered gristmill. During the course of his life, Deardorff watched Dover grow from a small frontier outpost to a booming canal town.

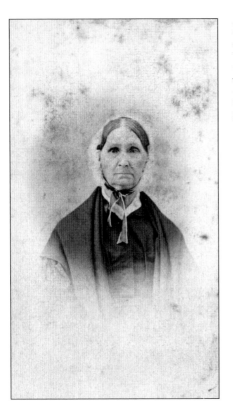

Margaret Butt Deardorff was the daughter of one of Dover Township's earliest settlers. Her father, William Butt, purchased 1,200 acres of land on July 1, 1809. She married Dover's founder, Christian Deardorff, in 1817. Shortly after their marriage, Christian built a new home for his bride on Front Street in Dover. She died in 1876.

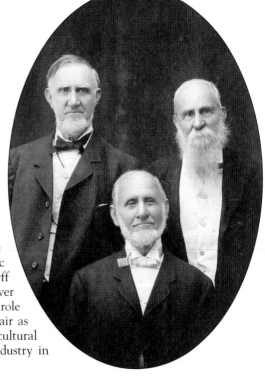

Pictured are three sons of Christian Deardorff. From left to right are George Deardorff, Upton Deardorff, and Isaac Deardorff. George founded the G. B. Deardorff and Son Hardware. Upton owned the Dover Salt Company and played an important role in the growth of the Tuscarawas County Fair as president of the Tuscarawas County Agricultural Society. Isaac worked in the mercantile industry in both Baltimore, Maryland, and Dover.

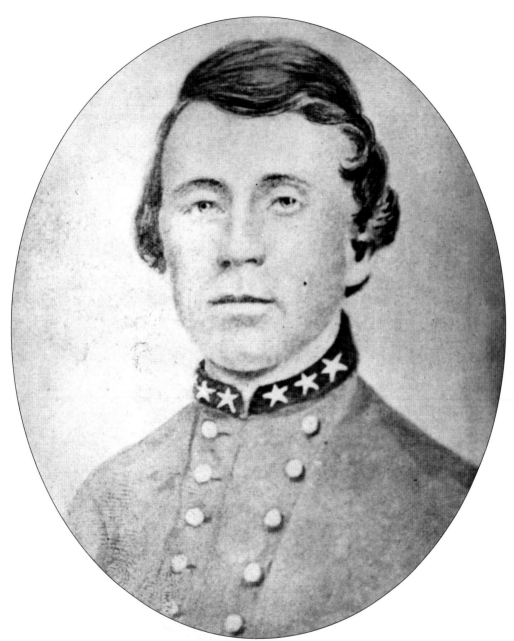

Pictured is William Clarke Quantrill, who was born on July 31, 1837, in Dover and educated in the local schools. Fighting for the Confederacy during the Civil War, he developed a national reputation for his ruthlessness. Quantrill's father, Thomas, was Dover's first school superintendent. Shortly after his father's death in 1854, Quantrill moved west, spending time traveling the western frontier in what is today Kansas, Missouri, Wyoming, Colorado, and even Salt Lake City, Utah. After the outbreak of the Civil War, Quantrill joined the Confederate side, serving first as a captain and later as a colonel. His most infamous act was a raid on Lawrence, Kansas, in 1863. During the raid, Kansas's capital city was burned to the ground. Two years later, Union troops cornered Quantrill in Kentucky and mortally wounded him. He died a month later on June 6, 1865.

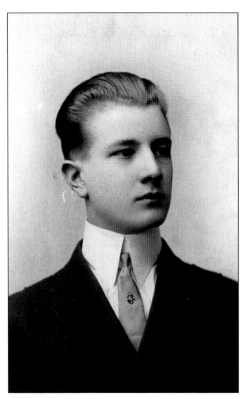

Elliot Nugent was born in 1896 at the Oaks, a stately home located on Tuscarawas Avenue. While attending Ohio State University, he met James Thurber, and they developed a lifelong friendship, collaborating on many projects, including Nugent's best-known play *The Male Animal*. Nugent wrote or cowrote 20 plays, directed 30 movies, and starred alongside stars such as Kathryn Hepburn, Bing Crosby, and Bob Hope. He died in 1980.

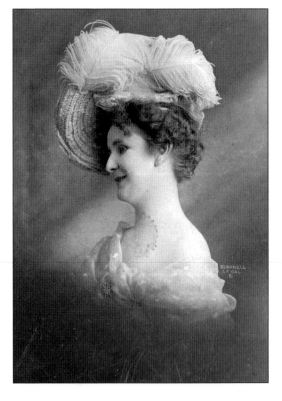

Norma Lee, wife of Nugent, was an accomplished actress of the 1920s, starring alongside her husband in the 1929 movie *Wise Girls*. The couple met in 1921 when they appeared together in the Broadway play *Dulcy*. They were married the same year.

On the night of May 28, 1880, an argument broke out between Ellen Athey (below) and her servant girl Mary Seneff (right). The impetus of the argument was Athey's suspicion about Seneff's relationship with her husband. During the argument, Athey grabbed an axe and struck Seneff multiple times. To cover up her crime, Athey buried the body in an ash pile behind her home. Later, after enlisting the help of her brother Alex Crites, they dumped the body in the Tuscarawas River. When Seneff's remains were discovered, Athey was identified as the prime suspect in the murder. During her trial in February 1881, Athey was found guilty and sent to the Ohio State Penitentiary. She was later found insane and committed to the Ohio Asylum for the Criminally Insane in Lima. She died there in 1920.

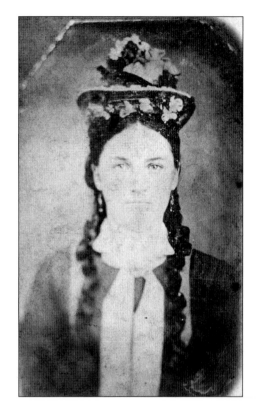

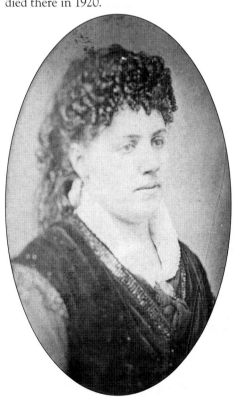

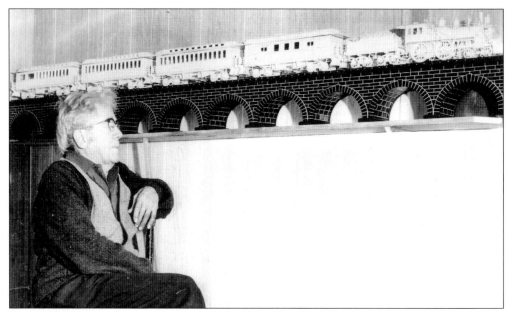

Ernest Warther was born on October 30, 1855, to Swiss immigrants. In 1899, he began work at the American Sheet and Tin Plate Company, serving the company for the next 23 years as a shearsman. At the age of 28, Warther went from a casual whittler to a serious carver. He continued carving until his death at the age of 87 in 1973. (Tuscarawas County Historical Society.)

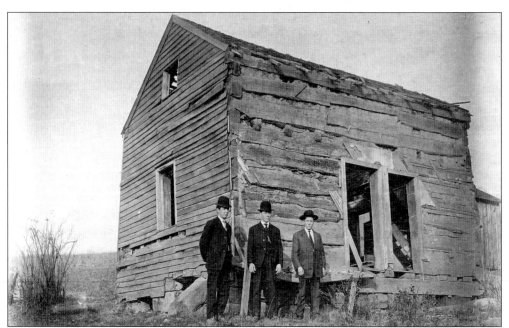

Pictured from left to right are Fred, Jake, and Ernest Warther at their birthplace on Dover Hill. As a child, Ernest received the nickname "Mooney" after the Swiss word for "bull of the herd." His first carvings were done with a pocketknife he found in a field. Later a hobo taught him to carve his trademark pliers. The working pliers were carved entirely from one piece of wood using only 10 cuts.

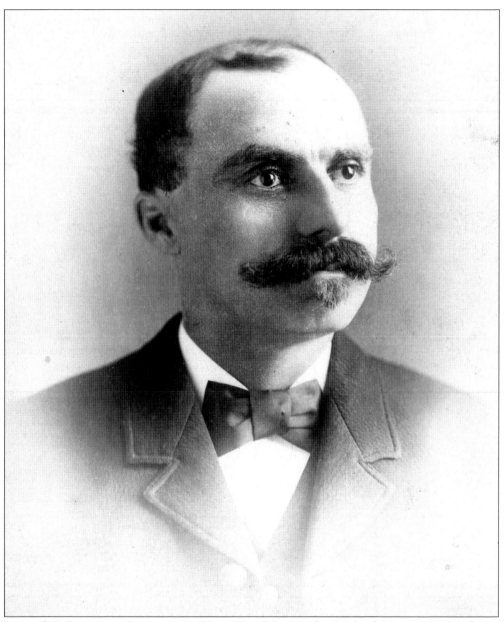

Jeremiah E. Reeves was born on June 23, 1845, in Montcombe, England. He was the fourth son of Albert George and Martha Reeves. When Jeremiah was just a young man, his father moved the family to Wales, taking a job in the local ironworks. At the age of 10, Jeremiah joined his brothers in the local ironworks, where he became skilled in boiler making and structural steel. After immigrating to the United States in 1867, he continued to work in steel. In 1869, he married Jane Rees in Connelsville, Pennsylvania. The couple had four children, a son and three daughters. In 1872, Jeremiah moved his family to Niles, where he and his eldest brother, George, established the Reeves Brothers Boiler Works. The business did well, and the opportunity arose for the brothers to purchase the struggling Dover Rolling Mill in 1883. Jeremiah remained in Dover for the next 37 years, establishing many successful businesses and supporting many charitable and civic causes.

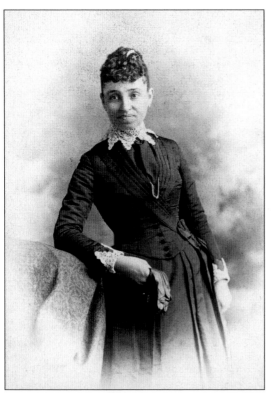

Jane Rees Reeves was born on January 20, 1847, in the small village of St. Clears, Wales. As a child, she immigrated to the United States and settled with her family in Connellsville, Pennsylvania. She was a devoted mother, wife, and member of the Moravian Church. She was confirmed at the Dover First Moravian Church on April 7, 1887. She died in Palm Beach, Florida, on March 6, 1926.

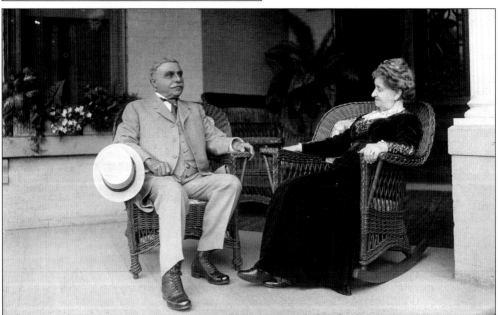

Jeremiah E. Reeves and his wife, Jane, relax on the front porch of their home. The luxurious wraparound porch was added during major renovations to the home in 1900. After the presidential elections of James Garfield in 1880 and William McKinley in 1896, the wraparound porch became a popular architectural element of homes. During the campaigns, both men refrained from traveling, delivering speeches from the comfort of their own front porches instead.

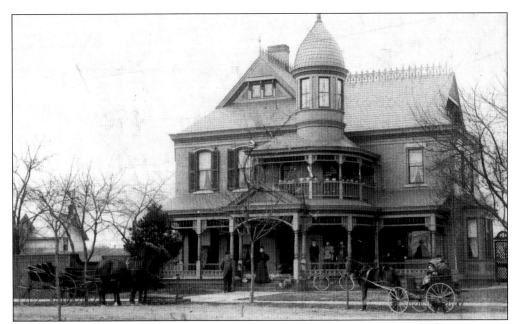

Before purchasing the Valentine Wills farmhouse, Jeremiah E. Reeves and his family lived in this grand home on West Sixth Street in Dover. Many days, Reeves was seen walking down Factory Street (Tuscarawas Avenue) to the Reeves Iron Works and home again well after midnight. Currently the Dover High School administration building parking lot sits where the home was situated.

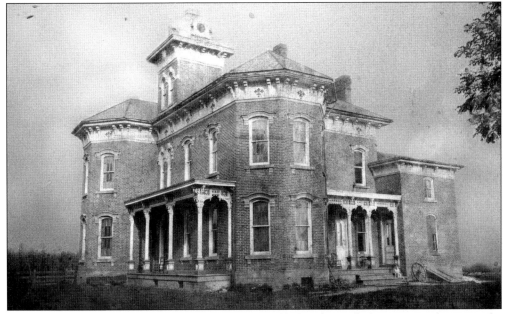

This is the only known image of the Valentine Wills farmhouse before its transformation by Dover industrialist Jeremiah E. Reeves at the dawn of the 20th century. The farmhouse was built in 1870 and occupied by various members of the Wills family. Reeves purchased the home and 400 acres of surrounding farmland, transforming it from the Italianate style to the newly popular Queen Anne style.

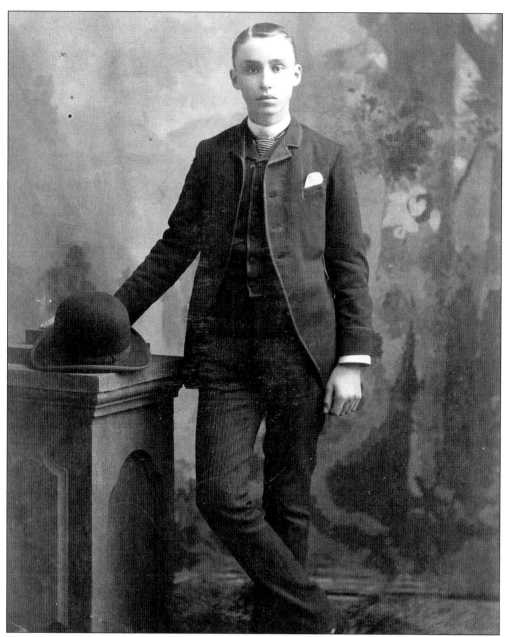

Samuel Jeremiah Reeves was born on September 14, 1870, in Connelsville, Pennsylvania. He was the first of four children of Jeremiah E. Reeves and Jane Rees Reeves. As a youth, he attended the public schools in Niles and Dover before joining his father in business. By the late 1890s, Samuel was running the businesses, with his father acting in an advisory role. It was Samuel who oversaw the sale of the Reeves Iron Works to the American Sheet and Tin Plate Company and the founding of the Reeves Manufacturing Company. In 1893, Samuel married Belle Croxton and the couple lived in a grand home on West Sixth Street in Dover. In 1901, at the young age of 30, Samuel contracted typhoid fever and died. At his funeral, he was remembered as "a quiet unostentatious, methodic, far-seeing man with a faculty for 'grasping the situation' and with untiring energy." Some even referred to him as a "coming Carnegie" for his business acumen.

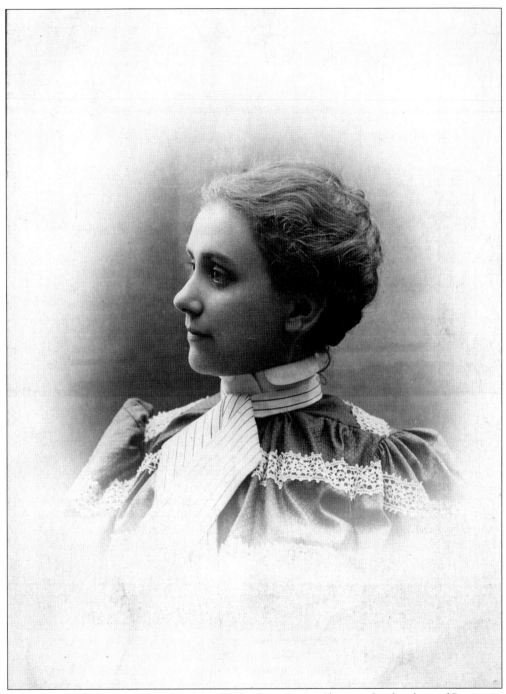

Belle Croxton Reeves was born on May 13, 1870, in Dover. She was the daughter of Benjamin Franklin Croxton and Clara V. Deardorff Croxton. Belle was a lifelong member of the Moravian Church and a descendant of Dover's founder, Christian Deardorff. Belle and Samuel Jeremiah Reeves had three children before his untimely death in 1901. Their children were Margaret Jane Reeves (born in 1894), Helen Florence Reeves (born in 1896), and Samuel Jeremiah Reeves Jr. (born in 1899).

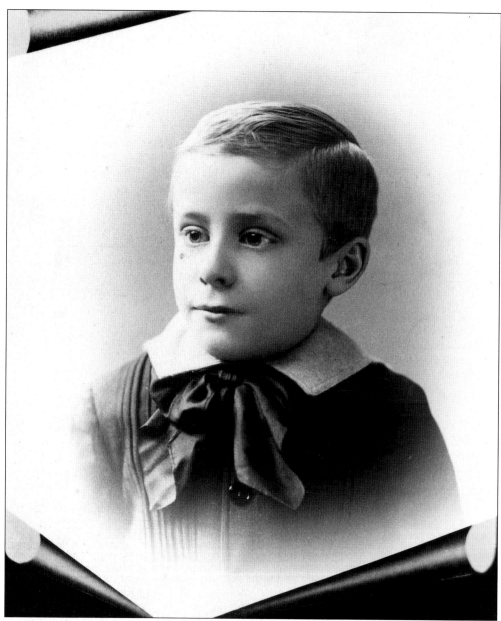

Samuel Jeremiah Reeves Jr. was born on April 10, 1899, in Dover. Throughout his life, Reeves was involved in the businesses created by his father and grandfather. He operated the Reeves Manufacturing Company through its many transitions. He retired from Empire-Detroit Steel in 1973 but continued as the director of the Cyclops Corporation until his death. He was also closely associated with the Reeves Banking and Trust Company, where he served as vice chairman. Among Reeves's many charitable interests was the Reeves Foundation, which he created and served as a trustee until his death in 1977. Since its inception, the Reeves Foundation has invested in many worthwhile community projects and organizations. Reeves married Margaret Hostetler Wagner in 1967. He was an active member of the Dover First Moravian Church, giving generously for the construction of the Reeves Library at Moravian College in Bethlehem, Pennsylvania.

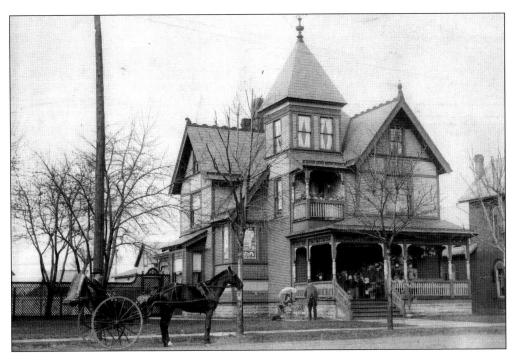

The home of Samuel Jeremiah Reeves Sr. was located at 219 West Sixth Street in Dover. This picture, taken in the 1890s, shows him in the carriage on the left. Today the home is used by the Dover city schools as the administration building.

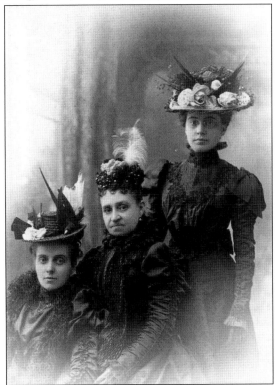

Lillian Reeves Fernsell, Jane Rees Reeves, and Louise Reeves Scheffer are all dressed in the elaborate style popular at the dawn of the 20th century.

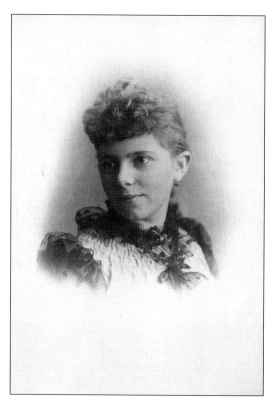

Agnes Reeves, middle daughter of Jeremiah and Jane Reeves, was born on August 7, 1880, in Niles, Ohio. In 1908, she married industrialist Herbert C. Greer in the front parlor of the Reeves family home on Iron Avenue. From an early age, Agnes took an interest in business and began work as a cashier at the Reeves Banking and Trust Company before her marriage. She had one child, Jane Greer, born in 1918.

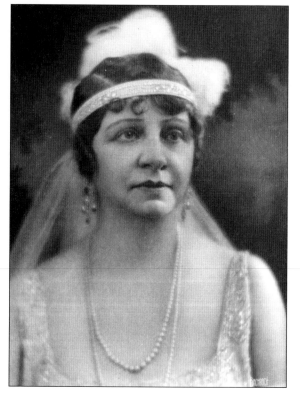

Agnes's ideas and innovations were well ahead of her time. She owned and founded several radio stations, including WJER in Dover, whose call letters were chosen in honor of her father, Jeremiah E. Reeves. Outside of her interests in the media, she served as president of Greer Limestone Company and the Greer Steel Company. An accomplished inventor, Agnes held 18 patents at the time of her death in 1972.

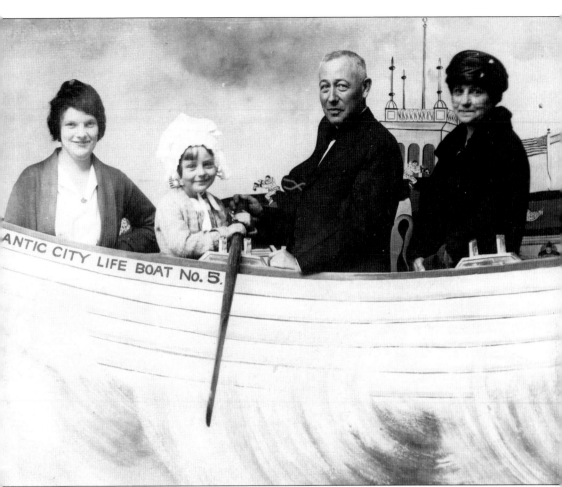

Pictured are Herbert C. Greer, Agnes Reeves Greer, their daughter Jane Greer, and an unidentified woman (far left). Herbert was born on August 11, 1877, at Sharon, Pennsylvania, and married Agnes in a private ceremony at her parents' home on June 3, 1908. Herbert was an astute businessman, operating coal and limestone interests in the Deckers Creek valley region of West Virginia and steel mills in Ohio and Indiana. Locally, he organized the Greer Steel Company in 1918.

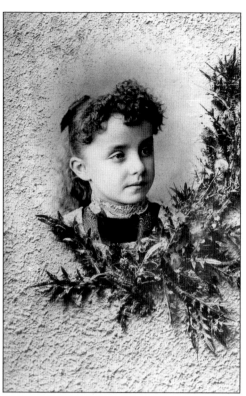

Lillian May Reeves was born on March 5, 1883, in Niles. On September 5, 1912, she married Charles Conrad Fernsell in Bournemouth, England. The wedding was kept secret from all but the closest of the couple's friends and family. After Reeves had been abroad for a few weeks, Fernsell traveled to England and the two were married. The couple had one child, Charles Conrad Fernsell III, born in 1918.

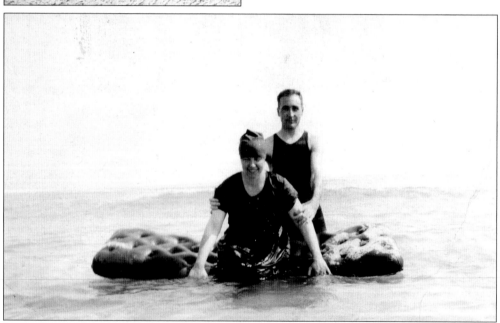

This photograph was taken while Lillian May Reeves and her husband, Charles Conrad (C. C.) Fernsell, vacationed. Fernsell was an attorney with the firm of Wilkin, Fernsell, and Fischer in New Philadelphia. He also served as vice president of the Reeves Banking and Trust Company, president of the Toledo, Fostoria, and Findlay Railroad Company, and director of the Reeves Manufacturing Company.

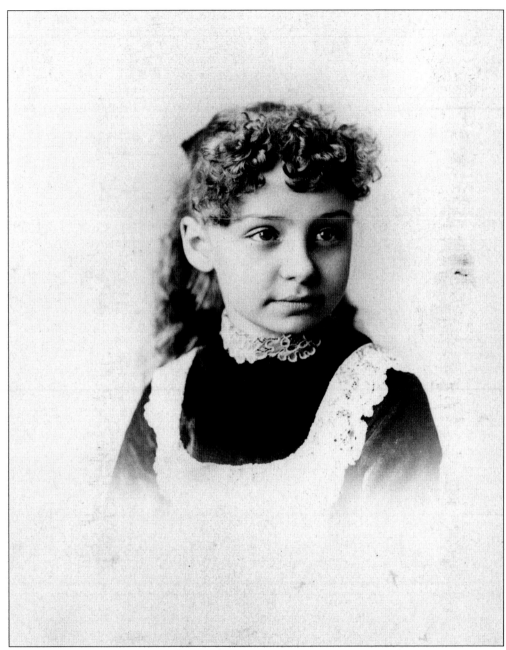

Louise Martha Reeves was born on June 8, 1875, the second child and first daughter of Jeremiah E. and Jane Reeves. She married Otto E. Scheffer at the Reeves home on East Iron Avenue on May 18, 1904. The couple had one son, Thomas Reeves. Sheffer and his brother-in-law Henry Worm operated Worm and Scheffer undertakers and furniture dealers in Dover. Worm handled the undertaking side of the business, while Scheffer focused on furniture sales.

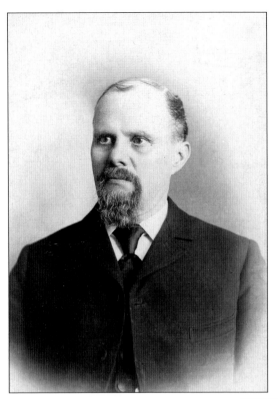

Jabez Reeves was born on August 3, 1840, to Albert George and Martha Reeves. In 1883, when the Reeves brothers purchased the struggling Dover Iron Works, Jabez moved to Dover to serve as the general superintendent of the mill. While his younger brother Jeremiah was known for his administrative talents, Jabez was regarded as the "blue collar" Reeves. Jabez and his wife, Mary Ann Jenkins, lived on Front Street in Dover.

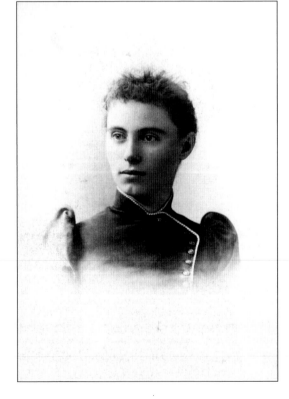

Mary Ann Jenkins was born on August 24, 1850, in Bryn Mawr, Monmouth, Wales. She and Jabez were married on July 6, 1868, in Newcastle, Pennsylvania. She loved music and met Jabez as a member of a Welsh singing group in Youngstown. After moving to Dover, she became an active member of the Dover First Moravian Church. The couple had five children.

Robert McCluney was Dover's second police chief and served the city from 1905 to 1907. He was born in Ireland in 1862 and first appears in local records in the 1890s. The McCluney family was not new to law enforcement. McCluney's uncle Gordon McCluney was a night watchman known for walking his beat accompanied by his dog. In the early 1900s, it was considered tradition to have an Irish cop.

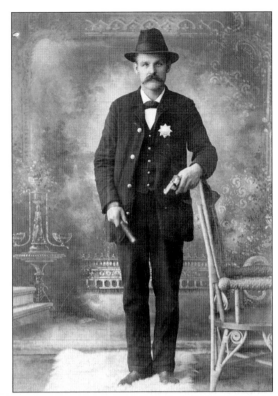

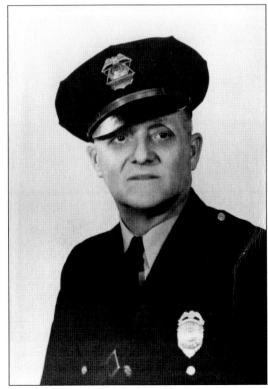

Frank H. Javens was named Dover's police chief on May 23, 1930, and served the city of Dover until March 31, 1957, when he retired. Under his guidance, the Dover Police Department increased in size from 5 officers to 11 officers and 2 dispatchers. Javens remains the longest-serving police chief in the city, having held the post for 27 years.

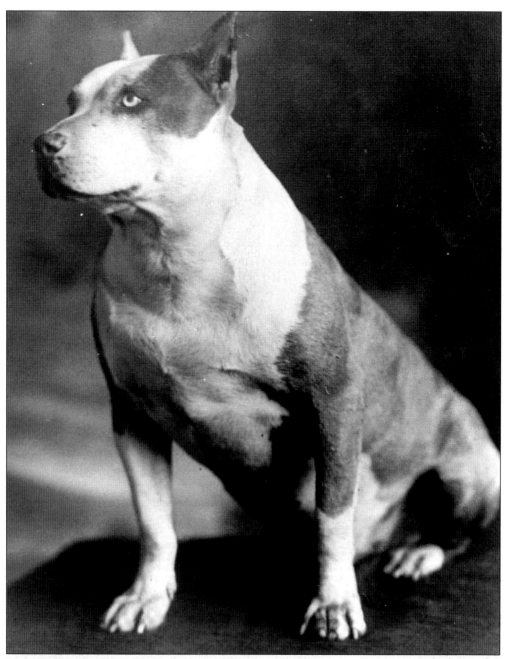

In the early 1920s, Dover fire chief Henry Geib began bringing his dog Grafter to the fire station. Over time, the dog became the official mascot of the department. For their amusement, the firemen would catch rats, release them, and Grafter would retrieve them. The dog was given his name by Geib, who claimed that a grafter was what one was called "if you stay at City Hall."

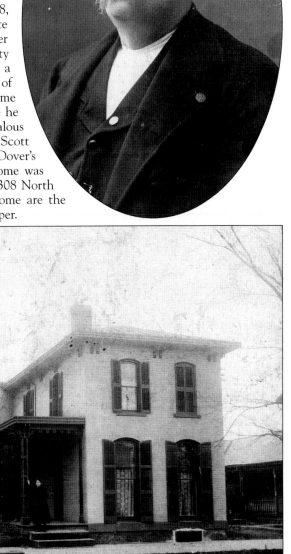

W. W. Scott was born on March 7, 1838, in Dover. In 1861, he enlisted as a private in Company G of the 16th Ohio Volunteer Infantry. He was discharged for a disability in 1863 but immediately reenlisted as a hospital steward with the 12th Regiment of Regulars. After the war, in 1879, he became editor of the *Iron Valley Reporter*, where he was well known for his outspoken and zealous approach in reporting the news. In 1898, Scott left the newspaper business and became Dover's postmaster. He died in 1902. Scott's home was located just off the square in Dover at 308 North Wooster Avenue. To the rear of the home are the offices of the *Iron Valley Reporter* newspaper.

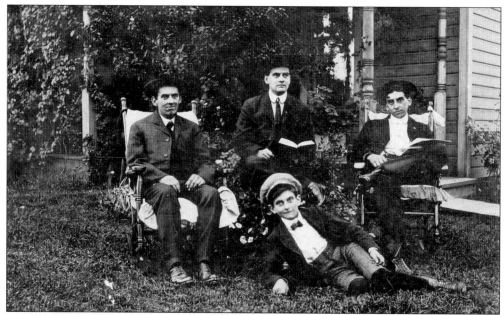

Pictured are the Rausch brothers. From left to right are Jacob Rausch, Alvin Rausch, Harry Rausch (front), and George Rausch. Three of the brothers went on to influential roles in the community. Alvin and his son Eugene operated a grocery for many years, Harry was a conductor on the Northern Ohio Traction and Light Company and later the manager of the A&P tea store, and Jacob worked as a carrier for the post office.

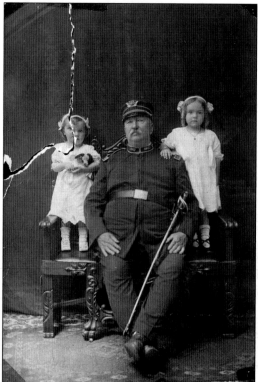

Pictured is Edward J. Horn, son of Jacob Horn and Caroline Baker. Jacob owned coal mines and helped build the Big Four Opera House in 1890. In 1892, he purchased and renovated the Horn Block in downtown Dover. After his father's death, Edward carried on the family businesses located in the Horn Block, including a restaurant, bakery, and a saloon.

A. B. Klar was born on April 17, 1872, and was a well-known proprietor of a fine grocery store. His grandfather came to Dover in 1844 and was employed to help dig the Calico Ditch but died of pneumonia the same year. Klar's father was a cooper who became a successful farmer and had 12 children. Klar attended local district schools before studying bookkeeping at the Scio College.

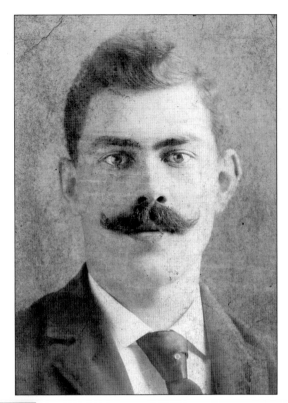

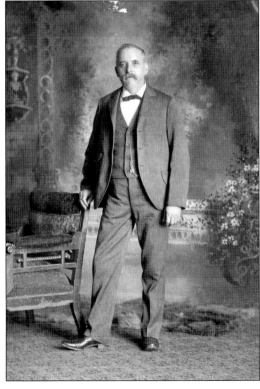

Gottlieb Krebs was born in Wattenwyl, Canton Bern, Switzerland, in 1853 and came to the United States in 1874. That year, he moved to Dover and established a jewelry store on Third Street.

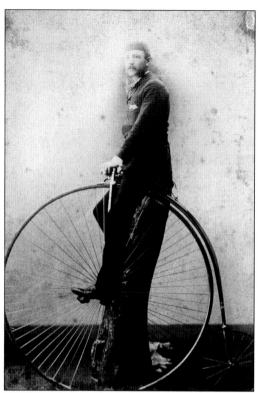

Pictured is Dover banker and bicycle enthusiast Charles F. Baker. Baker's father, Philip, founded the Exchange National Bank in July 1867. It was Dover's first bank, and Charles and his brother Jesse oversaw operations for many years. It was Charles who took a risk on young Jeremiah E. Reeves in 1883, loaning him the money to purchase the struggling Dover Rolling Mill.

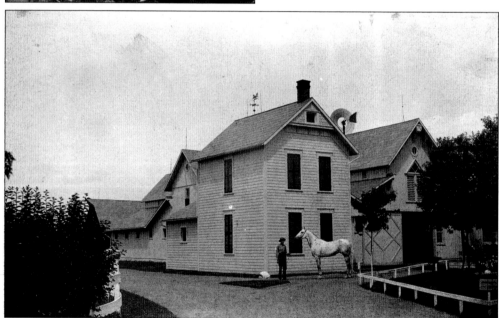

The Samuel J. Toomey stock farm was located between West Sixteenth and West Twentieth Streets in Dover. The farm featured a half-mile track where Toomey trained racehorses and tested all his carriages and sulkies. The farm measured 146.5 acres and stretched from North Wooster Avenue all the way to the Sugar Creek. Pictured in front of the barn is horse trainer Allie Walters.

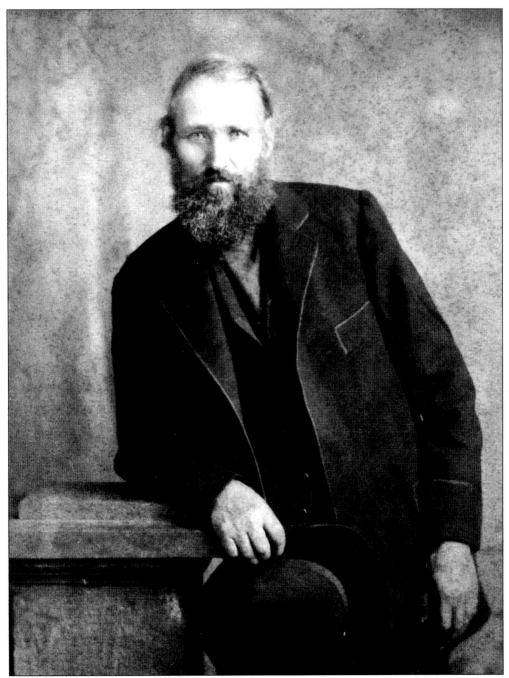

Around 1870, New Philadelphia farmer Valentine Wills decided to build an Italianate farmhouse on the land he owned between Dover and New Philadelphia. Wills was born on September 3, 1824, in Licking County but spent much of his life living in New Philadelphia. The Dover farmhouse was his residence for a short period of time while he constructed a new home in New Philadelphia. Like his Dover home, the residence on East High Avenue near the entrance to State Route 250, still stands. After Wills moved back to New Philadelphia, his son Charles Henry lived at the home in Dover. Wills died on January 3, 1894.

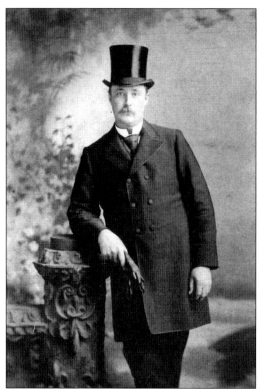

Charles Henry Wills was born on December 20, 1858, the first child of Valentine Wills and his second wife, Sarah Furney. Born in New Philadelphia, Charles later oversaw his father's Dover farm, which was sold to Jeremiah E. Reeves in 1900. Charles married Bell B. Miskimen on April 24, 1883, and died on September 8, 1939, at the age of 80.

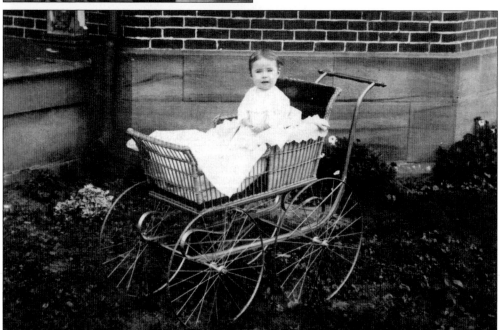

This image, taken around 1890, shows Nellie Virginia Wills, age two, in front of the Wills farmhouse at 325 East Iron Avenue. She was the daughter of Charles Henry and Bell B. Miskimen Wills. This is one of only two images that exist of the home before Reeves purchased it in 1900.

Two

DOVER SCHOOLS, SPORTS, AND CHURCHES

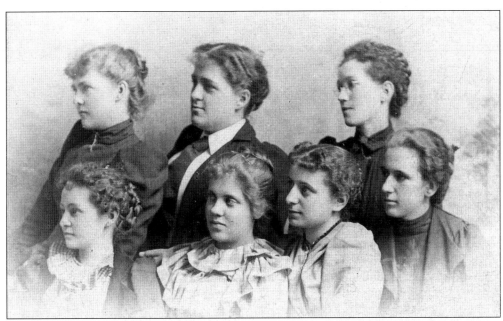

Pictured is the faculty of Dover's Second Street School for the years 1892 to 1894. From left to right are (first row) Ada Zimmerman, Gertrude Adams, Ida Leiser, and Anna Notter; (second row) Eldora Holmes, Edith Scott, and Mary Pollock. Notice the young age of most of the teachers, as prior to 1900, it was not unusual for teachers to be the same age or even younger than their students. Because of the agrarian way of life in Tuscarawas County, many young men only attended school during the winters and took longer to graduate then their female counterparts. This created the possibility of a 20-year-old male student taught by a 19-year-old female teacher.

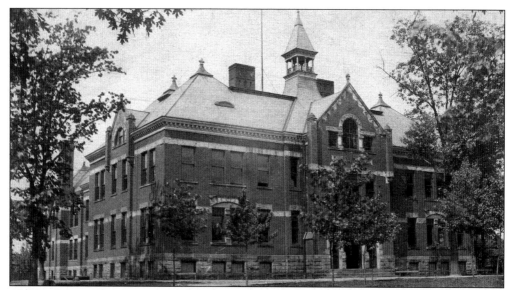

The land for Oak Grove School was acquired from Henry Hayden, who had lived in a large residence on the site. The school received its name for the beautiful grove of oak trees that Hayden cultivated on his property. In 1878, Dover schools purchased Hayden's property for $6,000. Before it was a private residence, the area was used for the first county fairs.

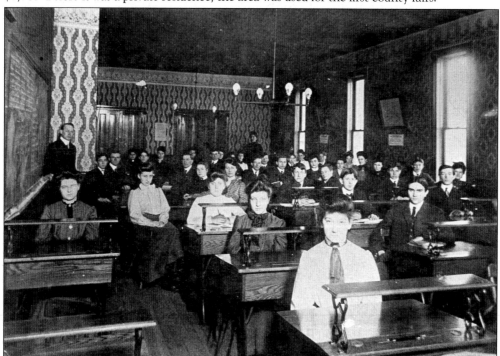

Pictured are students at Dover's Oak Grove School in the 1890s. Oak Grove School was built in 1889 and 1890 on Walnut Street in Dover. The school was located on the West Sixth Street side of the land where the present Dover High School sits today. The school remained in operation until 1938 when, due to overcrowding and opportunities presented by Pres. Franklin D. Roosevelt's New Deal, it was torn down.

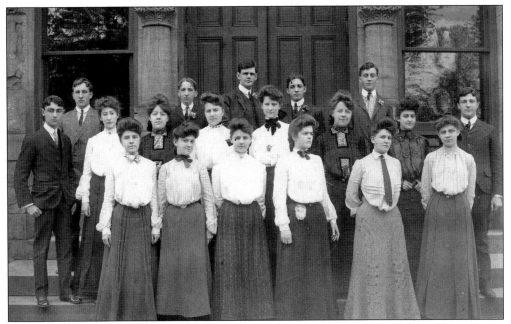

This photograph of Dover High School's class of 1904 was taken for the *Cleveland Plain Dealer* on May 20, 1904. Pictured are Edith Kraus, Viola L. Peters, Anna Mae Geltz, Myrtle Bryan, Mame Snyder, Florence Ripple, Felix Warren Hoffman, Carrie Lewis, Grace Brannon, Marie Krantz, Treva Wallick, Helen Brannon, Irene Strickmaker, Archie A. Weiss, C. Ross Weber, Ed Rinderknecht, Joe Hostetler, Elden Steitz, and Edgar C. Davis.

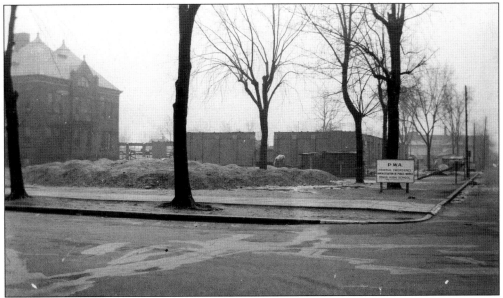

In 1938, Dover's Oak Grove School was razed and construction began on a new high school to connect with the existing Roosevelt High School on Fifth Street. The new Sixth Street addition was constructed as a Public Works Administration project under the New Deal and cost $800,000. When it was completed, the new school housed six elementary grades and a six-year high school.

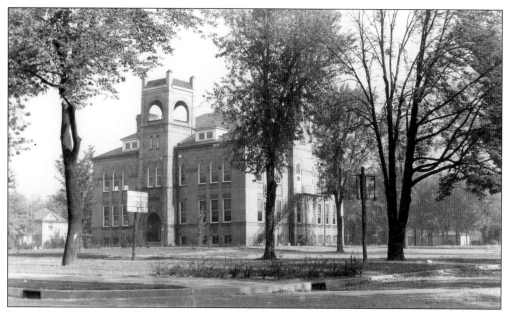

Dover's Second Street School was constructed of wood in 1868 but later extensively renovated with a brick edifice added to the exterior of the building in 1883. In 1884, Dover's high school was located on the third floor of the building. High school students attended the Second Street School until Oak Grove School was built in 1889.

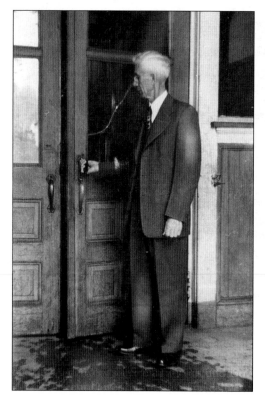

Second Street School was located at the head of East Second Street on the site of the old Crater homestead. By the time it was razed in 1952, the school was severely outdated and lacked many modern conveniences, including inside toilets. On the school's final day, October 20, 1952, its principal of 38 years, O. L. Youngen, symbolically closed the door on the school for the last time.

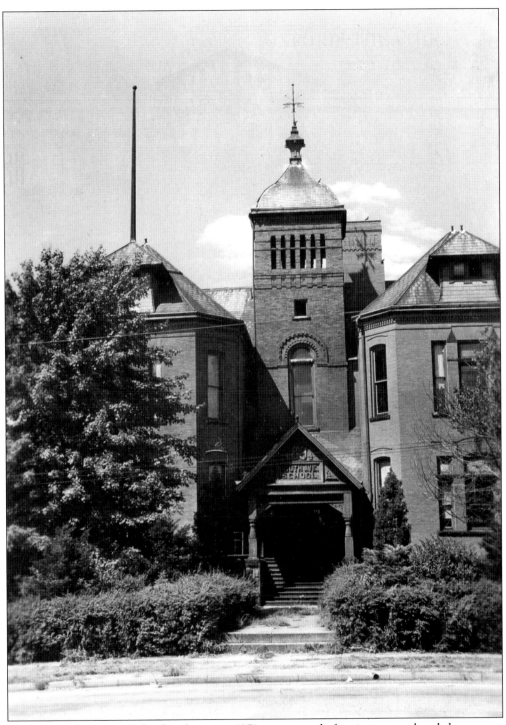

Dover's South Avenue School is shown in 1951 just a year before it was razed and the current South School was built. South Avenue School was constructed in 1894 as an elementary school that served the children living south of the Tuscarawas River. The South Avenue School was located between Shafer and South Avenue on Union Avenue.

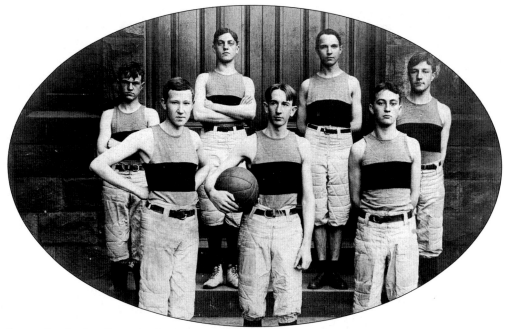

Pictured is the first Dover basketball team in 1903, with Charles Teters holding the ball. In 1901, Teters came to Dover from Mount Union College and organized Dover's first basketball team. Although he was part of the faculty, he acted as both a player and a coach. The team played and practiced at the old Beller skating rink on West Second Street.

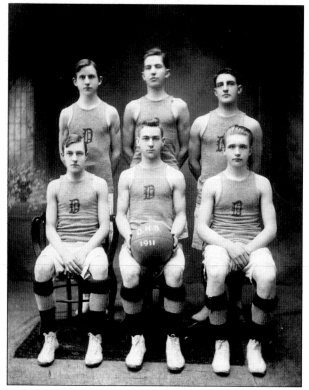

Pictured are members of Dover's 1911 basketball team. From left to right are (first row) Clifford "Rinky" Reiss, Ernie Godfrey, and Walter Brucks; (second row) Harry Winkler, Claude Herzig, and Ernest Peter. Later Brucks partnered with his brother Ferdinand to operate Brucks Brother's Hardware at 221 West Third Street.

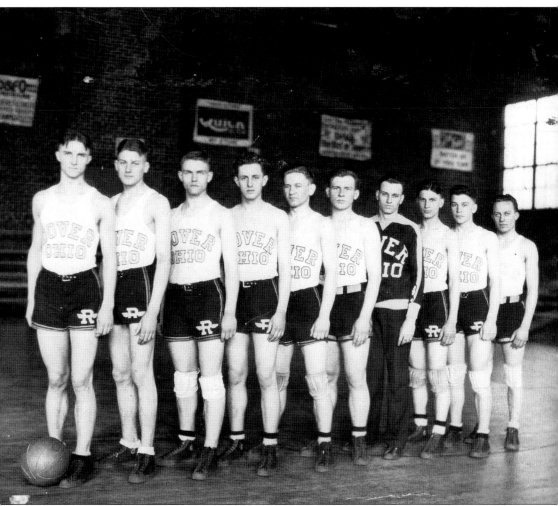

The 1927 Dover basketball team was the first squad to bring a state championship to town. During the regular season, they compiled a record of 17-5 before winning four games in the eastern Ohio district tournament and another three games in the state tournament to bring home the title. A week later, the team traveled to Chicago to compete in a national tournament. They were victorious against Kansas City but fell in their second game to Colorado Springs. Pictured from left to right are Frank Slaughter, Carl Braun, Bill Beitner, Art Schlundt, Ted Yorkevitz, Dwight (Ike) Trubey, coach Joe Hermann, Raymond Low, Herman "Bup" Rearick, and Ralph Buehler.

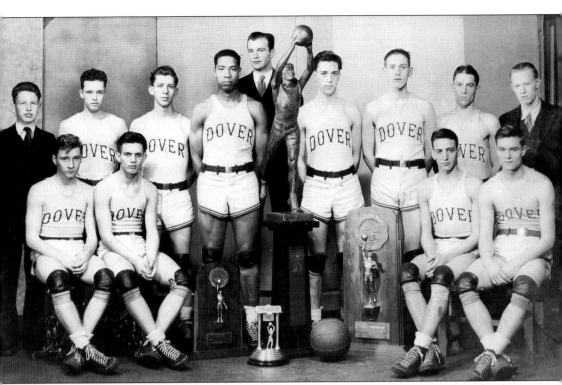

Dover's 1932–1933 basketball team won the second state championship for the school in six years. Pictured from left to right are (first row) Edgar "Bud" Davis, Richard (Dick) Klar, Harold "Braunie" Braum, and Earl Maurer; (second row) manager Robert Swinderman, Dale Andeas, Harry "Sonny" Seribert, Frank "Doc" Kelker, coach Herman "Bup" Rearick, Robert (Bob) Boyd, Tom Homrighausen, Donn Godfrey, and manager Herb Davis. Donald "Pop" Goettge is not pictured. Rearick went on to compile one of the highest winning percentages in school history. During his coaching tenure from 1931 to 1937, he compiled a record of 51-13-4.

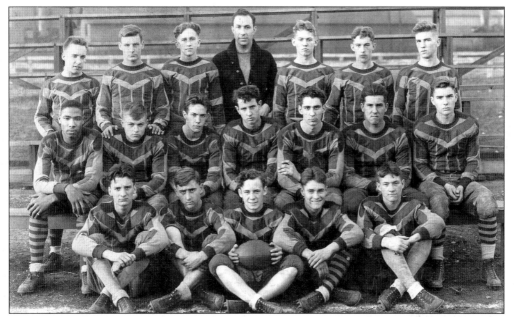

The 1930 Dover Crimsons football team compiled a record of 4-4-2 and was named county champs. Pictured are (first row) Herb Kaufman, Russ Graves, Jim Gano, Earl Maurer, and Fred Souers; (second row) Doc Kelker, Albert Hartman, Don Foutz, Woody Herman, William Schleiper, Eugene Horn, and Trevor Rees; (third row) Tom Mason, Jim Smith, Ray Lindamood, coach Gus Peterka, Dale Godfrey, and Marion Archinal.

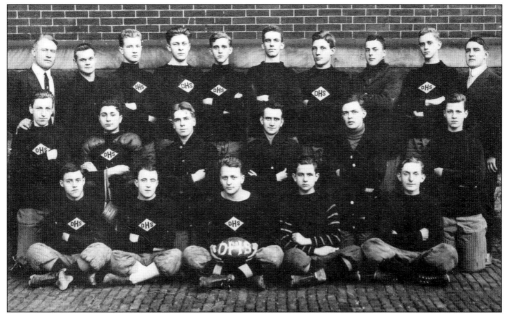

Pictured is the 1913 Dover Crimsons football team that compiled a record of 2-4-1. Prior to the 1930s, the team was referred to as the Crimsons for the color of their uniforms. In one of their losses, the Dover team forfeited with only 2 minutes and 45 seconds left. They left the field in protest of their opponent's dirty tactics and the poor officiating. Pictured third from the left in the back row is Elliot Nugent.

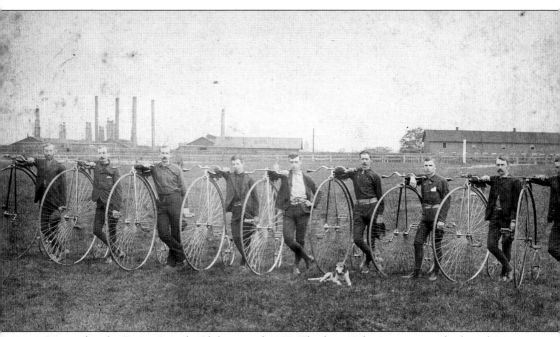

Pictured is the Dover Bicycle Club around 1887. The late 19th century saw the bicycle craze in Tuscarawas County reach its peak, as local residents formed "wheeling clubs." To capitalize on this craze, a tax was established to create bicycle lanes at the side of public roads. The tax was $2 and applied to anyone who wanted to ride on the city's roads. Many objected to the tax for the reason that the bicycle lanes would only be built on roads between the major towns. Interest in bicycling peaked in Tuscarawas County during the summer of 1899 when the county fairgrounds hosted a two-day state meet.

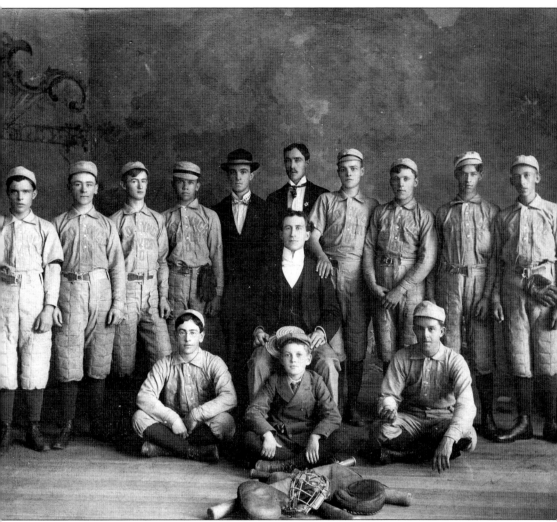

Pictured is a Dover baseball team sponsored by W. D. Lynch on January 23, 1904. Lynch operated a dancing school in the Vinton Block of downtown Dover. During the 1890s, baseball became America's national pastime, and teams began playing all over Tuscarawas County. Every town had sandlot baseball fields, and many contests were scheduled between cities. By 1906, the Tuscarawas Valley Baseball Association was founded. The association leased land from the city at Merchants Park and picked its team from the local stars of Dover, New Philadelphia, and Strasburg. The new association's first game was scheduled for May 4, 1906, against Massillon.

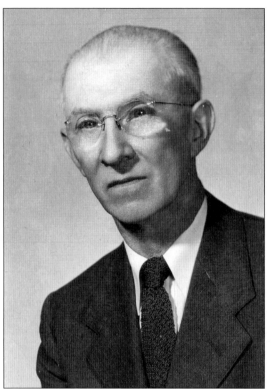

L. H. Alexander organized Dover High School's first orchestra in 1916 and put together the school's first band in 1917. The 1917 band was the first to don a uniform of white shirts and white duck pants. This remained the uniform until 1929, when the Women's Club of Dover lobbied for separate seasonal uniforms. In addition to his work with the band, Alexander also wrote Dover's fight song and alma mater.

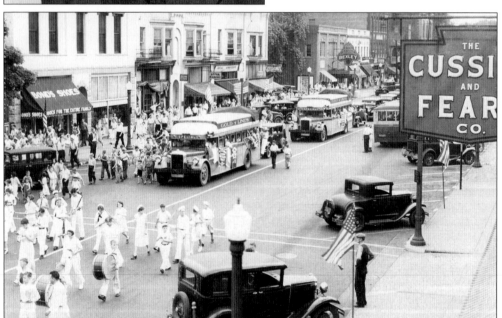

In 1933, Dover High School's marching band was named the national champions at a contest in Evanston, Illinois. Pictured is a parade through downtown to honor the band. It was the only representative from Ohio to attend the national band contest. The 76-member band was led by Alexander. After being honored with the national championship, the band performed at the 1933 World's Fair in Chicago.

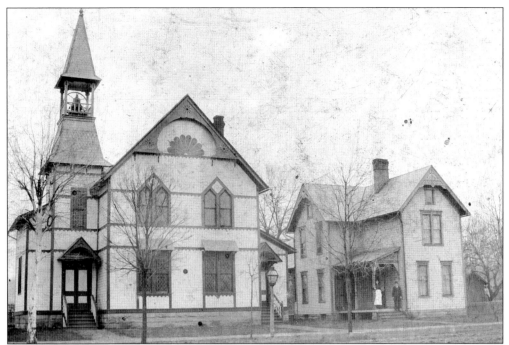

On September 16, 1836, 36 people met in a schoolhouse in Dover, forming an English Lutheran congregation. The new congregation joined together with the local German Reformed Church, purchased a lot, and built a parish that the two congregations could share. During the Civil War, the Lutherans sold their interest in the jointly owned church and purchased a building from the United Brethren Church just off Dover's square.

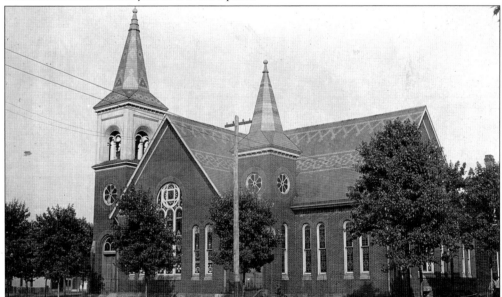

The English Lutheran Congregation worshiped in the old United Brethren Church until 1890, when the building was demolished and a new one was constructed at the same location, 108 West Third Street. On June 1, 1890, the cornerstone was laid for a new church (pictured), which remained in use until the current Grace Lutheran Church was dedicated in 1959.

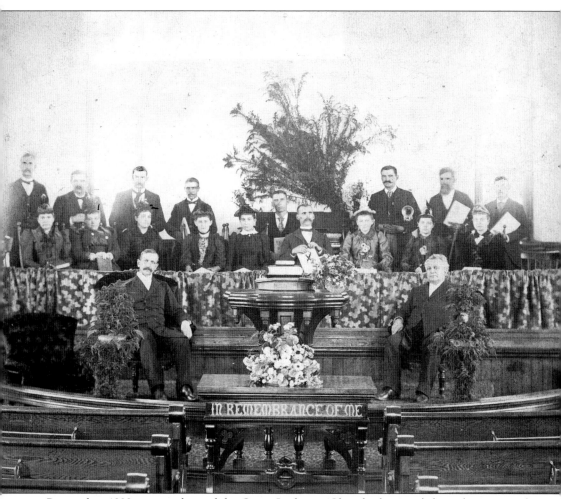

Pictured in 1893 are members of the Grace Lutheran Church choir and their clergy just a few years after the dedication of their 1890 building at 108 West Third Street. Included are (first row) Reverend Breitenbaugh and Reverend Wiles; (second row) Mrs. Lafayette Myers, Mrs. John Strickmaker, Mrs. John Kerch, Ruby Keplinger, Elizabeth Burkle, Stella Bryan, and Edith Bomgardner; (third row) Frank Baer, George Bryan, Homer Keplinger, Benjamin Lawrence, Samuel Mansell (director), Fred Sliffe, Mr. Keplinger Sr., and Lafayette Myers.

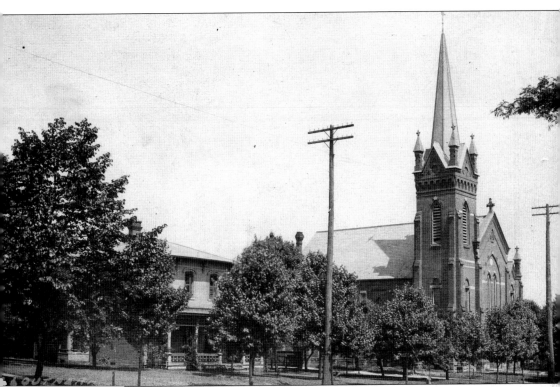

In 1838, members of the German Lutheran congregation and the English Lutheran congregation joined together to build a shared house of worship on the corner of Wooster Avenue and Fourth Street in Dover. Although the congregations remained separate, the two churches shared the building until the 1860s. After the end of the Civil War, the English Lutheran congregation dissolved the partnership and purchased a building near Dover's square. Members of the German Lutheran congregation continued in the original building until 1880, when a new brick church was constructed for $14,000. This building has sustained the congregation ever since. Later the German Lutheran congregation was renamed St. John's and affiliated itself with the United Church of Christ. The building was extensively renovated in 1938 and continues to support a strong congregation today.

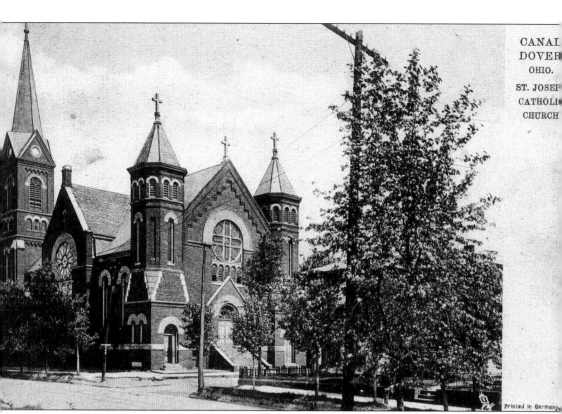

In 1849, ground was broken for St. Joseph's Catholic Church, and it was completed a year later. That building served the parish for the next 74 years, beginning as a church and later used as a schoolhouse. In 1898, the parish built a new church (pictured) across Tuscarawas Avenue. In the early 1960s, structural problems were found in the church that made the task of repairing the building impossible. The last mass was celebrated on September 30, 1962, before the building was razed to construct the current St. Joseph's.

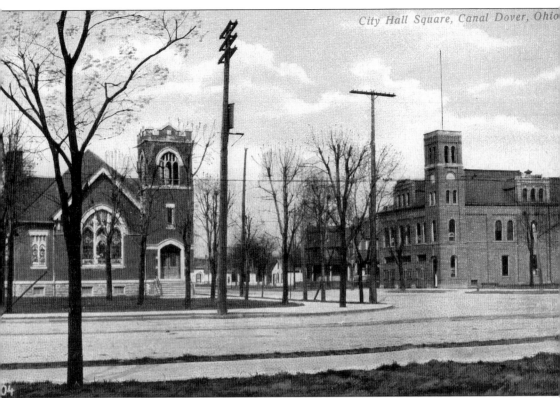

Dover's First Methodist Episcopal Church was born out of the circuit riders of the early 19th century. Circuit riders were preachers on horseback who traveled the country to spread the gospel. In the summer of 1832, local followers of the Methodist Episcopal denomination proposed the construction of a church at Dover, and in 1833, a simple one-story frame structure was constructed on the corner of Second and Race Streets. The original building underwent several renovations. In 1870, the building was sold to Dover carriage maker Samuel J. Toomey for $1,000, and a site was selected on the square in Dover for a much larger brick building. On June 11, 1905, the new church was dedicated. This remained the home of the Dover First Methodist Church until 1958, when a new structure was built at 1725 North Wooster Avenue. The Methodist church on the square in Dover was purchased by the Salvation Army in 1957.

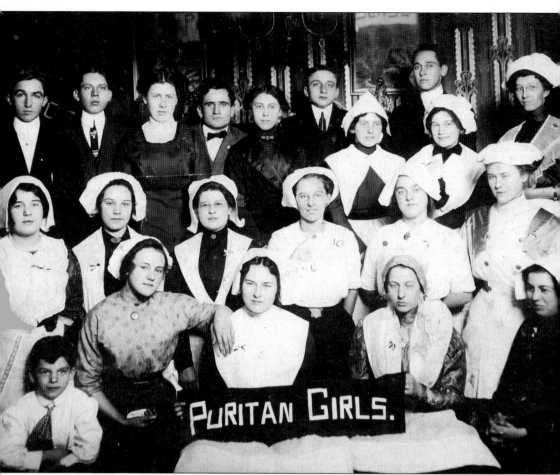

PURITAN GIRLS.

Here are Dover's First Methodist Episcopal Church Puritan Girls around 1910. In the late 19th century, many American churches began extensive missionary work, as they rediscovered the ideals of their Puritan ancestors. The Puritan concepts of "a city on a hill" and "an errand into the wilderness" once again became relevant, as organized efforts were made to Christianize foreigners, immigrants, and even Native Americans. As congregations celebrated their Puritan roots, they put on programs and skits in celebration of the past. The image above may be of one of these programs.

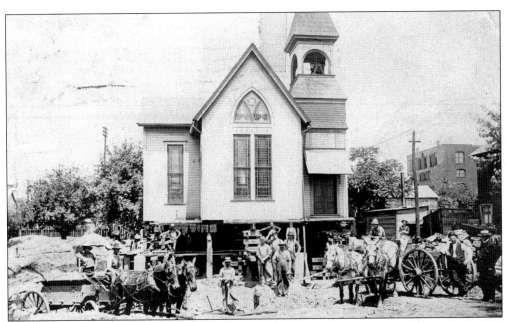

The Dover First Moravian Church was organized in 1842, and its first church was built in 1843. In 1892, renovations were made to the original building, adding a bell tower, removing the balcony, and reorienting the sanctuary. In 1898, the church building was moved from one end of the congregation's property to the other, a distance of approximately 20 feet. Here the church remained until it was razed in 1909.

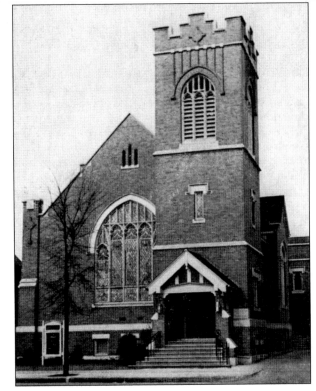

The 1909 Dover First Moravian Church is home to a Moeller organ, which was made possible by a $1,000 gift from the Carnegie Foundation, and an Echo organ, given by Jeremiah E. Reeves and his wife, Jane. In 1991, the church was extensively remodeled with another reorientation of the sanctuary, new classrooms, offices, and a fellowship hall.

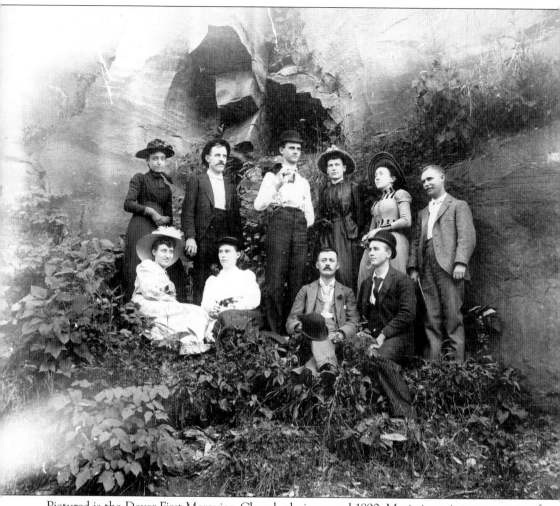

Pictured is the Dover First Moravian Church choir around 1890. Music is an important part of the Moravian heritage. Prior to the Revolutionary War, the Moravian Church founded the first white settlement in Tuscarawas County at Schoenbrunn. Their history and music are forever intertwined in the history of the early years of Tuscarawas County. Pictured are members of the choir at Harger's rock. From left to right are (first row) Ada Meyer Bigler, Anna Arnold White, Otheo Weible, and Fred Reese; (second row) Emma Harger, Charles Geiser, Hager Ricksecker, Mary Wassman, Carrie Harger, and Fred Arnold.

Three

BUGGIES, TRAINS, TROLLEYS, CARS, AND CANAL BOATS

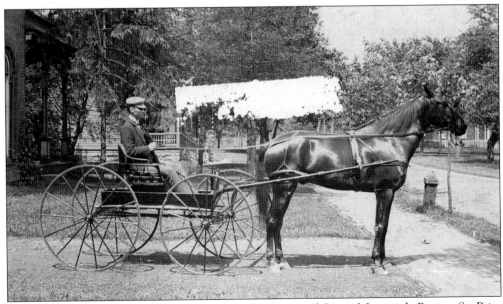

Pictured are the driver, horse, and high-wheeled buggy of Samuel Jeremiah Reeves Sr. Prior to the era of the automobile, horses and buggies were commonplace on Dover's city streets. High-wheeled buggies were considered fast and dangerous and were usually driven by men. The high-wheel construction was helpful in an era without paved roads, where deep wheel ruts could play havoc on carriages.

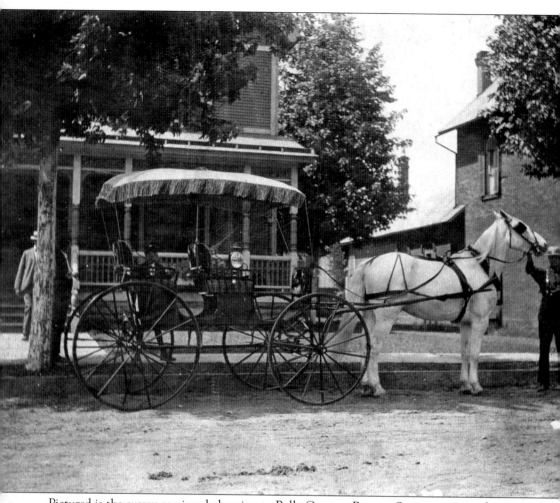

Pictured is the surrey carriage belonging to Belle Croxton Reeves. Surrey carriages first arrived in the United States in 1872 and were very popular during the late 19th and early 20th centuries. Their unique design featured two seats, open sides, and a canopy top. This particular one has a fringe top. Fringe-top surreys were later immortalized by Richard Rodgers and Oscar Hammerstein in their musical *Oklahoma*. The show, opening in 1943, featured the musical number "The Surrey With the Fringe on Top."

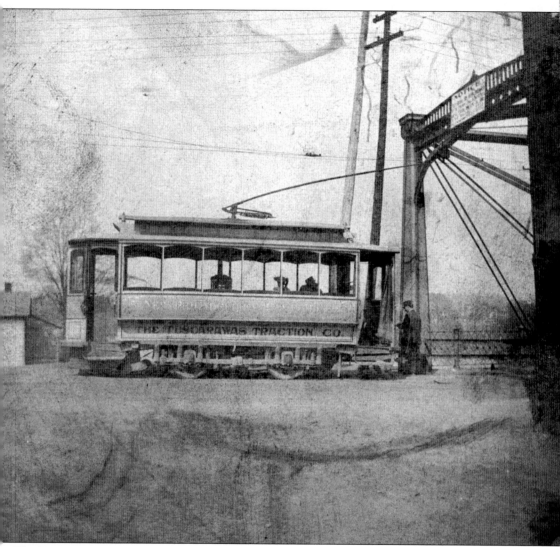

The Tuscarawas Traction Company was the brainchild of Tom L. Johnson. Despite the relatively small population of Dover and New Philadelphia, Johnson felt that an electric railway would be useful because of the proximity of the two towns' business districts. Work began in 1889, and on July 4, 1889, the first car made the trek from the barn at West Seventh and Factory Streets in Dover to the square in New Philadelphia. Originally Johnson had hoped to install a turntable on the square in New Philadelphia, but when the men attempted to construct it, they were arrested and jailed overnight. As a compromise with the city, a turntable was constructed a few blocks past the public square on the corner of East High Avenue and Ninth Street in New Philadelphia. In 1906, the Canton-New Philadelphia Company, owners of the Tuscarawas Traction Company, merged with the Northern Ohio Traction and Light Company.

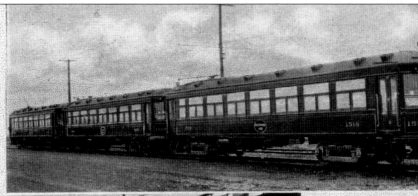

RIDE THE
INTERURBAN
Hourly Limited
Service between
Akron—Canton
Cleveland.

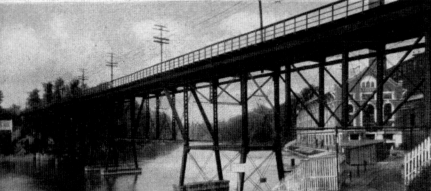

No Dirt
No Dust
No Cin

Comfortal
Courteo
Servic

THE NORTHERN OHIO TRACTION & LIGHT CO.

The Northern Ohio Traction and Light Company merged with the Canton-New Philadelphia Company and several smaller streetcar lines to form a regional interurban train network. On April 29, 1906, the first train arrived in Dover and New Philadelphia from Canton. Local lines existed on both Tuscarawas and Wooster Avenues. The merger of these independent lines successfully connected Cleveland, Akron, Canton, Dover, New Philadelphia, and Uhrichsville. After 23 years, the Northern Ohio Traction and Light Company ceased operations due to the growing preference for the automobile. Local service ceased in 1929, and the company was out of business completely by April 1932.

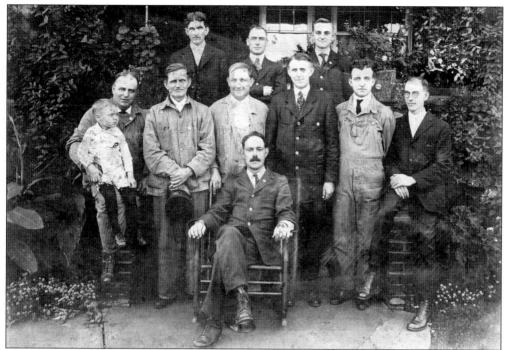

Pictured are employees of the Northern Ohio Traction and Light Company in 1921. From left to right are (seated) William Bayless, a conductor for the streetcar line; (second row) Herbert Patton (with an unidentified boy), Joe McCartney, W. E. Zimmerman, Edward Peacock, Bill Seggett, and Roy Cox; (third row) Albert Hamilton, Harrison Wolf, and Orrin Mohn.

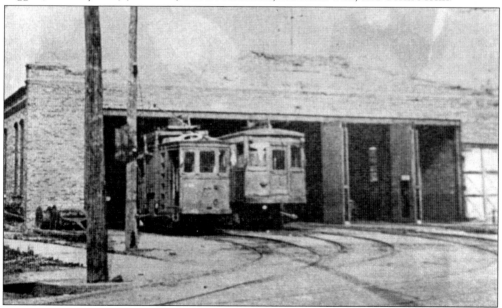

The streetcar barn was located on the corner of East Tenth Street and North Wooster Avenue. It was built in 1903 by the Canton-New Philadelphia Company and used as the northern connection of the Tuscarawas Traction Company. In 1906, the Tuscarawas Traction Company was purchased by the Northern Ohio Traction and Light Company.

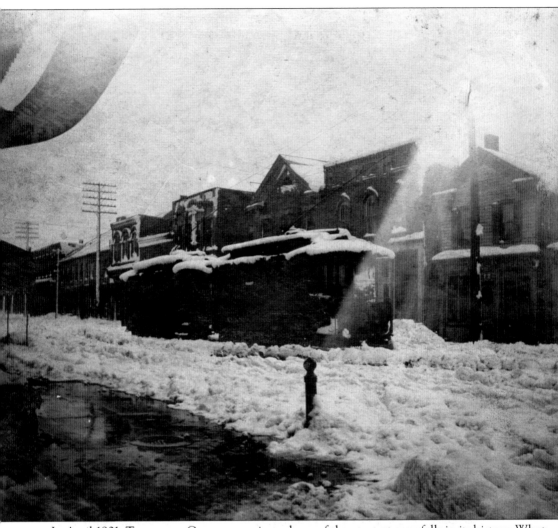

In April 1901, Tuscarawas County experienced one of the greatest snowfalls in its history. What began as rain turned to snow and fell constantly for nearly three days. The heavy snowfall resulted in the loss of telephone lines, loss of electricity, and stopping of all streetcars. Streetcar service was not resumed until Sunday, April 20. Even then, streetcars ran through valleys of snow stretching four to six feet high on either side of the tracks. After the snow melted, problems remained for the Tuscarawas River valley, as flooding was experienced throughout the county.

In 1907, Jeremiah E. Reeves purchased his first automobile and began motoring around Dover. An automobile enthusiast, by 1913, Reeves had three cars, two electric and one gas powered, according to his tax records. By the time of his death in 1920, he owned six automobiles, including two Pierce Arrows. The Pierce Arrow was the official state car of Pres. William Howard Taft and Pres. Woodrow Wilson.

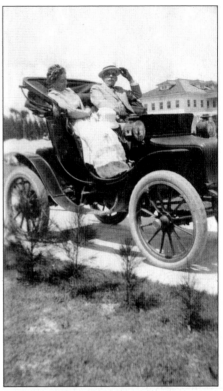

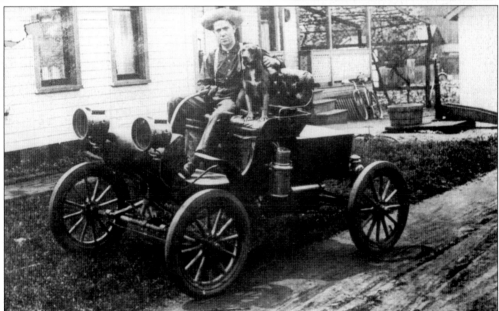

Pictured is Ernest "Mooney" Warther in his automobile around 1910. Like much of the rest of the country, Warther fell victim to the automobile craze in the early 20th century. Unlike most of the rest of the country, he eventually gave up on driving. In the late 1920s after several accidents, he sold his car and began riding his bicycle everywhere he needed to go. (Tuscarawas County Historical Society.)

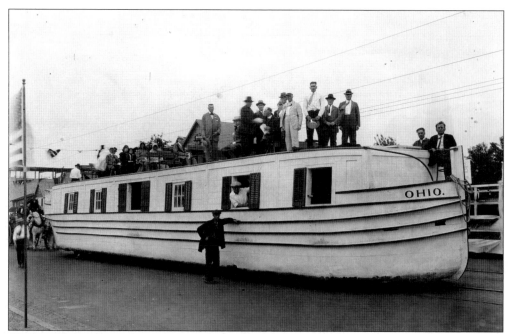

The canal boat *Ohio* is pictured on wheels for its part in a parade. The *Ohio* was a passenger packet used for travel. Riders paid 5¢ per mile, which included food and a sleeping berth. Passenger packets ran both day and night and could cover 80 to 100 miles per day. They carried up to 60 people and usually included the living quarters of the canal boat captain and his family.

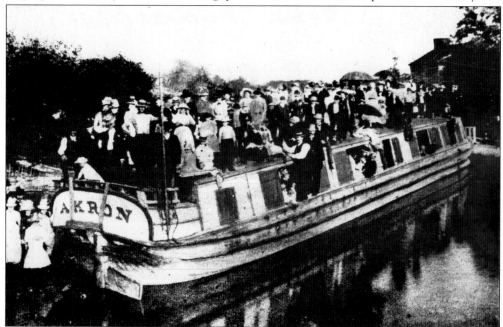

The canal boat *Akron* was owned and operated by Capt. J. Frank Lyons of Newcomerstown. The Ohio and Erie Canal was crucial to Ohio's development. It connected the Great Lakes with the Ohio River, opening up the fertile Ohio farmlands to markets in the south and the east. In the picture is a Methodist church group on a picnic outing in 1884.

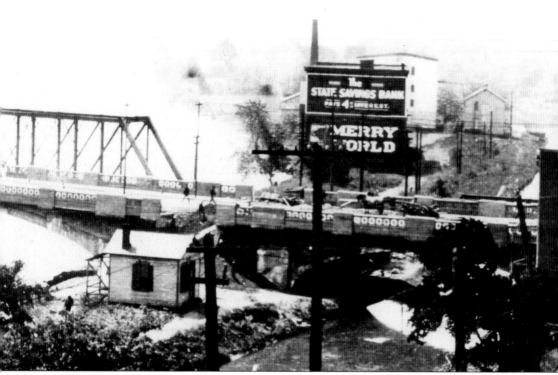

Prior to being filled in after the flood of 1913, the Ohio and Erie Canal went under the Factory Street bridge. In front of the bridge is the tollhouse. This was the only canal tollhouse in Tuscarawas County and a credit to Dover's founder, Christian Deardorff, who worked to secure the small building. Because of the tollhouse, boats backed up at Dover, creating a clientele for local inns, stores, saloons, and restaurants. In the background is an advertisement for the Merry World Tobacco Company, which made both smoking and chewing tobacco and was located in Wheeling, West Virginia. Just visible behind the Merry World sign is the Hardesty Milling Company.

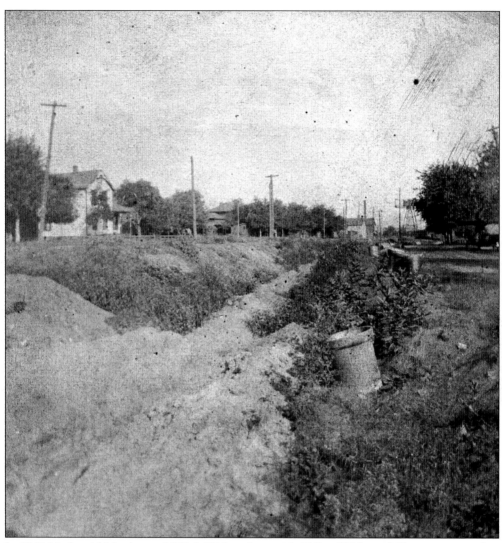

In 1843, Nathaniel Hayden and Elijah Welty, along with Keller, Hildt, and Company, joined to build a millrace between the Sugar Creek and the Tuscarawas River, a distance of three miles. The work of digging the ditch was difficult and expensive, taking its toll on the firm of Keller, Hildt and Company, which went bankrupt. The financial burden was great on the investors that remained, and they were forced to resort to paying the workers with merchandise from the store owned by Hayden and Welty. In response to this pay and low wages, the workers organized a strike, tying pieces of calico cloth around sticks and parading up and down Factory Street. Even after the strike was settled, the millrace was called the Calico Ditch.

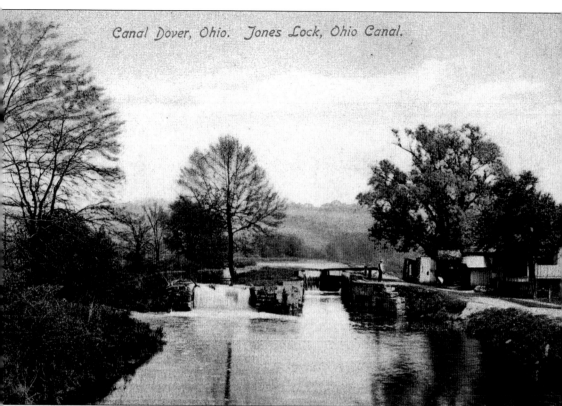
Canal Dover, Ohio.   Jones Lock, Ohio Canal.

Jones Lock is one of two locks located in Dover on the Ohio and Erie Canal. Lock 11 and Lock 12 (Jones Lock) were located just north along Route 800; Jones Lock was situated near Hillcrest Garden Center. At some point, the remains of Lock 11 fell into private hands and were used as the basement of a small home. In recent years, the house has decayed, and the old lock is now once again visible to anyone traveling along Route 800.

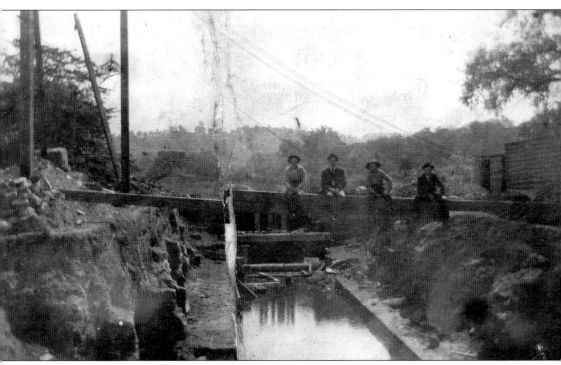

Between 1904 and 1907, the State of Ohio organized a major canal restoration project. The aim of the workers was to waterproof and reinforce the locks. As part of the process, the original sandstone blocks were covered by a layer of concrete. On many of the locks that remain today, this cement facing is still visible.

Four

DOVER BUSINESSES, BIG AND SMALL

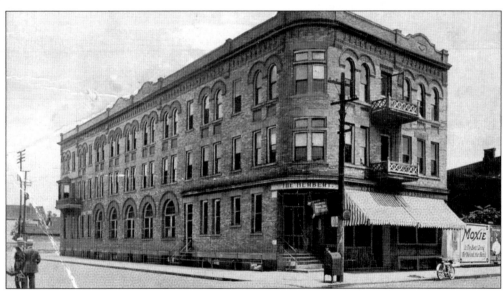

The Herbert House Hotel was founded by Dover resident Daniel Defenbacher in 1899 and opened to the public on July 10, 1900. Originally possessing 50 guest rooms, it was heated by steam and featured both gas and electric lighting. Although it was not connected to a bar, it did offer guests the luxury of fine billiard tables. A grand gala event was planned for the hotel's opening, as tickets were sold for $5 per couple or $3 for individuals. The ticket entitled the bearer to dinner, entertainment provided by an orchestra, and a distinguished speaker. Among those attending were Samuel J. Toomey, George Fertig, and Christian Deis. In 1906, Defenbacher sold the Herbert House Hotel to Christian Bernard, the brewer, who expanded it into a neighboring vacant lot, nearly doubling the total number of rooms. The hotel was located on the corner of Second and Factory Streets in Dover.

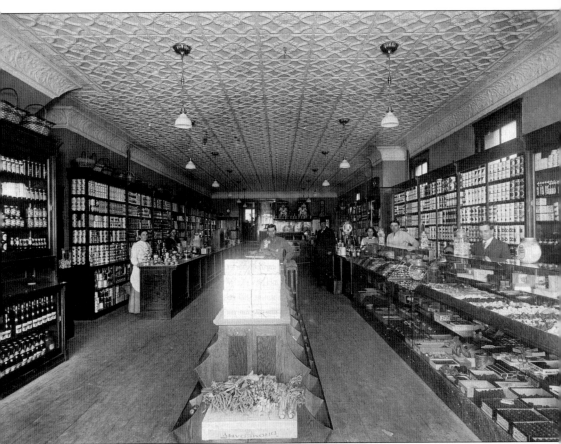

Pictured is the interior of the Rausch Grocery Store around 1914. Using the slogan "Rausch Your Grocer," the Rausch store became one of the best-known grocers in the area. The Rausch grocery was located at 119 West Third Street. Marie Rausch is pictured on the left, George Rausch is in the middle, and Alvin Rausch is on the far right. Alvin was the founder of the store, along with his wife, Marie. George worked at the store for a while before moving out of the area. Today the Renaissance Salon occupies the site of the Rauch Grocery Store. The original floor and tin ceiling are still visible.

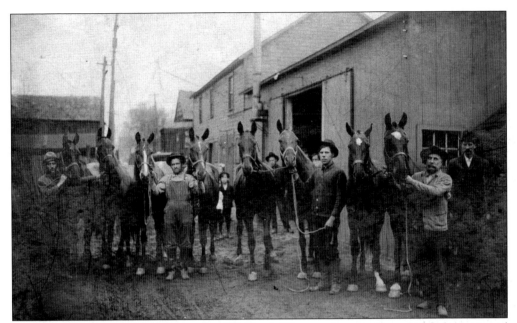

The Froelich Livery Barn was located at 216 North Wooster Avenue. Elmer Froelich is pictured on the right. In addition to operating his livery barn, Froelich, like many tradesmen, also lived at the site of his business. Livery barns provided board and exercise for the horses of local residents in exchange for a fee. This was very convenient for city dwellers who did not have stables of their own.

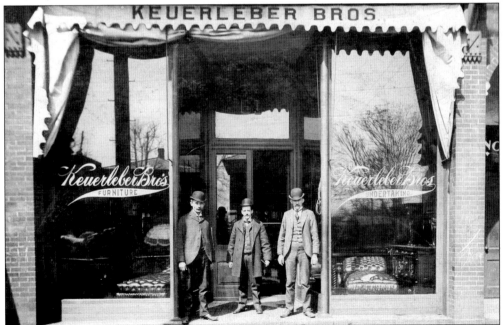

The Keuerleber Brothers Furniture Store was located at 222 West Third Street. In addition to the furniture store, the Keuerleber brothers, Henry and Christ, also served the community as funeral directors. During the late 19th and early 20th centuries, many furniture and cabinetmakers also constructed coffins.

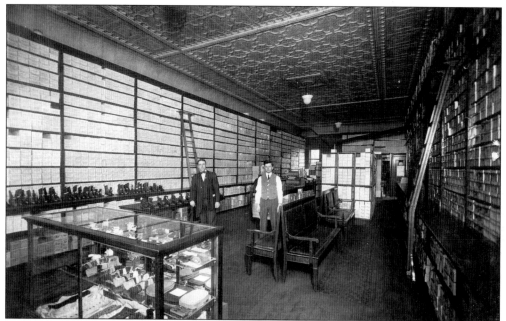

Both the home and business of Samuel Stettler were located at 216 Factory Street. The Stettler shoe store served the residents of Dover from the early 1900s until 1951. Stettler founded the store, and his sons Charles and Frank continued the business as Stettler Brothers after their father's death. The store sold and repaired shoes.

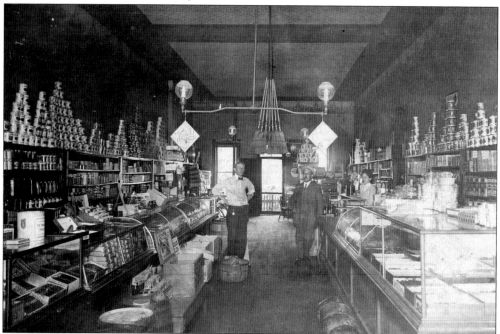

Pictured is W. G. Immel's Grocery, located at 203 West Third Street around 1909. Shown are clerk Pearl Rabe and salesman and owner, W. G. Immel. In addition to his grocery, Immel also operated a delivery service in and around Dover. He owned seven wagons used to deliver items for 18 different Dover businesses. The delivery service operated from 1910 until 1939.

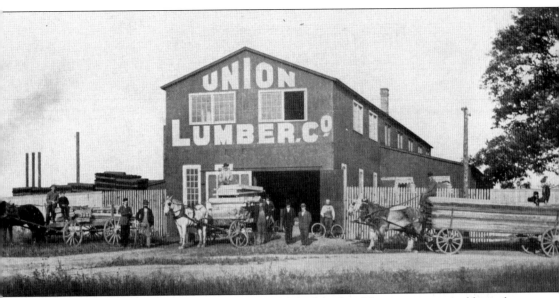

In 1903, the Union Lumber Company was established by local businessmen to address the community's need for a large lumberyard and planing mill. The company's first president was James Rees, a native of Wales and brother-in-law to Jeremiah E. Reeves. The Union Lumber Company employed many talented woodworkers, specializing in fine interior finishes, stairs, panel work, mantels, and office and bank fixtures. Beginning in August 1903, the Union Lumber Company in Dover developed a line of cement blocks used in the construction of many local buildings. The Union Lumber Company was located on Regent Street in Dover's Tin Town neighborhood.

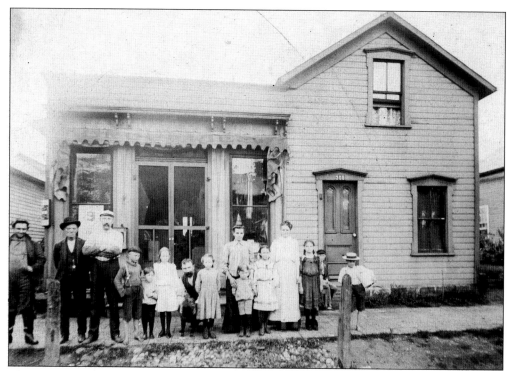

The Pretorious Grocery Store was located at 305 Front Street in Dover. The business was started by Valentine Pretorious in the early 1900s. The store served as both a business and a residence, with the entire family contributing to its success. During the 19th and early 20th centuries, neighborhood groceries were commonplace. In Dover alone there were 25 grocers operating within the city limits in 1907.

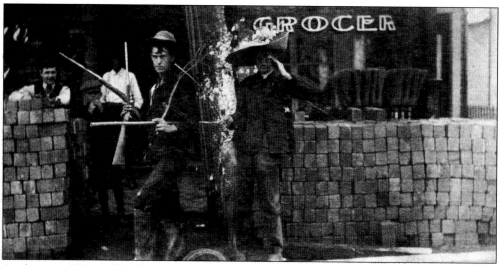

At the age of 22 in 1894, Dover resident A. B. Klar established his grocery store at 400 North Wooster Avenue. By the early 20th century, the grocery store was one of the most modern in the city. It boasted the best goods and prices and provided delivery to customers throughout Dover. Pictured are two young men playing outside Klar's store in 1906.

G. Krebs and Company Jewelry Store was located at 307 West Third Street. The store was opened in 1874 by Gottlieb Krebs and remained late into the 1940s. In addition to jewelry, the store specialized in eye exams and glasses. Krebs's son Charles worked at engraving and repairs, and his other son Walter, a graduate of Northern Illinois College of Ophthalmology, conducted eye exams and fitted clients with glasses.

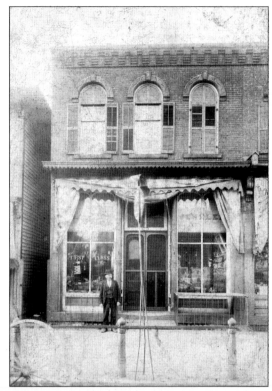

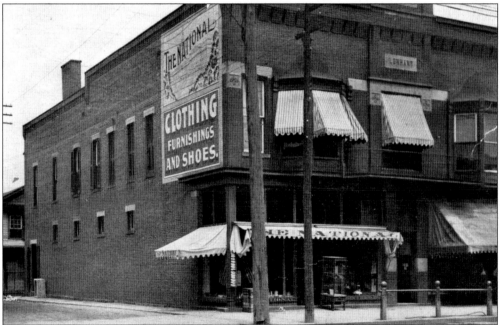

The National Clothing and Shoe Company was founded in 1902 by John Jurgens and Walter Scheu and opened on Factory Street in Dover. In 1905, it was relocated to the building pictured at 231 West Third Street. In its heyday, the store sold a variety of items for men, including clothing, shoes, hats, caps, trunks, and valises. Locals referred to the store simply as "the National."

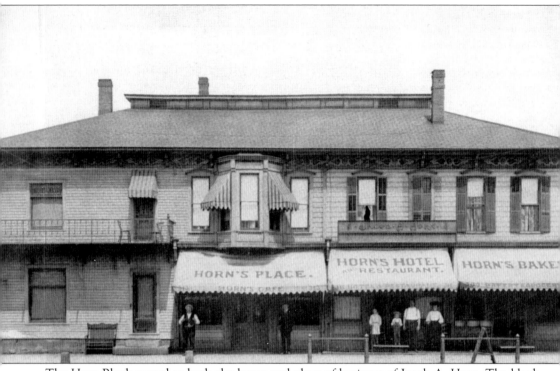

The Horn Block served as both the home and place of business of Jacob A. Horn. The block was located at 309–315 Tuscarawas Avenue. Horn was a prominent businessman in Dover at the end of the 19th century, playing an important role in shaping the downtown. In addition to the Horn Block, which was constructed in 1902, he was one of the four original owners of the Big Four Opera House and along with F. H. Waldron established the Tuscarawas Valley Brewing Company.

Charlie Fisher is pictured next to his scissors grinder in the 1890s. The scissors grinder was a fixture in small towns in the late 19th and early 20th centuries. These men carried their trade on their backs, sharpening scissors, knives, hedge shears, and small hatchets. To drum up business, they rang a bell as they walked. Fisher is pictured with his sharpening apparatus and bell.

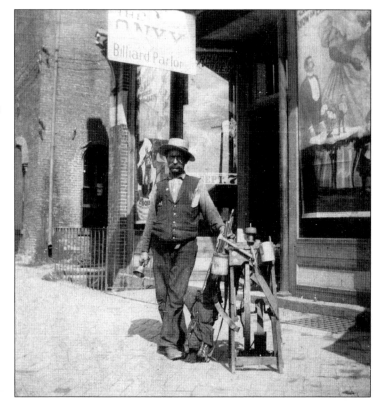

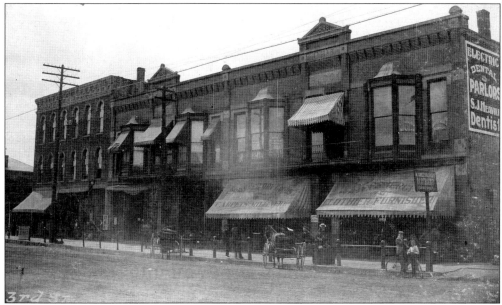

The Deis Building was located at 233–235 West Third Street and was constructed in 1888. Over the years, it housed many businesses, including the Tuscarawas Telephone Company, Davie's Dry Goods, E. Fienberg and Company women's clothing, and Buehla Morgan's Studio, where Morgan produced oil paintings. Prior to the construction of the new Tuscarawas County Senior Center, the previous senior center was located in the building.

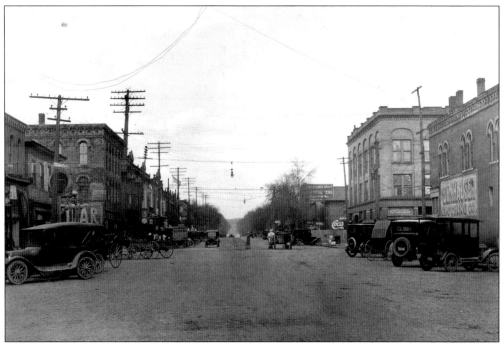

Photographed looking east from Factory Street toward the Dover square, Senhauser's clothing store is on the right. The store was founded by Norman and A. J. Senhauser and sold clothing, hats, and furnishings. It was located at 236 Factory Street on the corner of West Third Street.

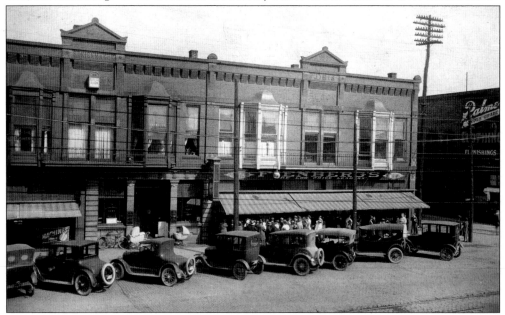

The 200 block of West Third Street featured the Strickmaker and Deis Buildings. Several 1920s businesses are pictured, including Fienberg's Discount Store, Harbaugh Photography, Dr. Earl Shaweker, Palmer Clothing and Furnishings, and the Exchange National Bank. The crowd gathered at Fienberg's leads one to believe that a sale is taking place. The Exchange National Bank was founded by P. Baker as Dover's first bank in 1867.

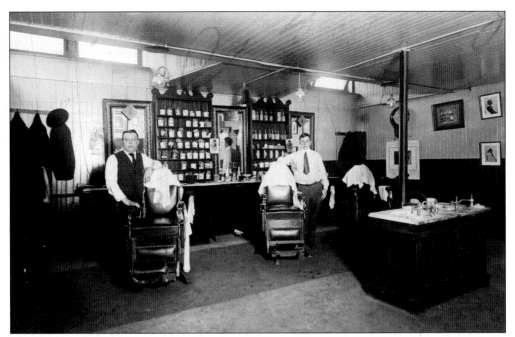

The Theiss and Jones Barber Shop (in the 1920s) was located at 236 Factory Street, sharing a building with Senhauser's clothing store. Edward Theiss is pictured on the left, and John Jones is on the right. At the time Theiss operated his barbershop, there were seven others in downtown Dover, including one operated by Edward Jentes directly across Factory Street.

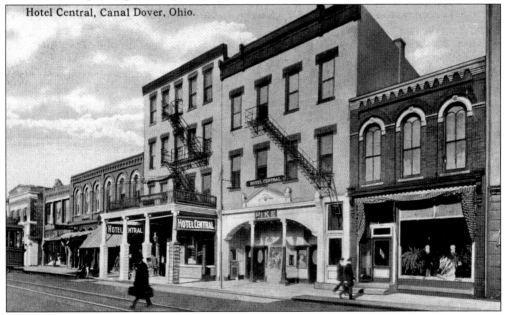

Dover's Central Hotel was in business over 50 years, beginning in 1857. Located at 209–211 Factory Street, the Central Hotel was purchased by Edward Horn in 1905. Horn extensively remodeled the property. When renovations were finished, the hotel contained 50 rooms, all of which were equipped with heat and a private bath. The building also featured a grand dining room and spacious parlors.

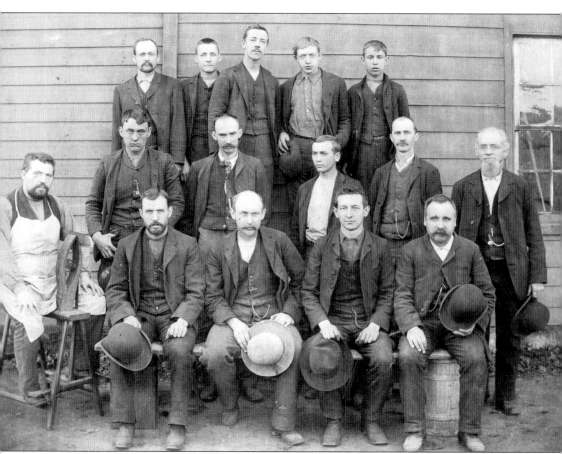

Shown are the employees of the S. Toomey and Son Carriage Manufactory established in 1868 by Samuel J. Toomey and operated at 125–131 East Second Street on the corner of Race Street. In the early years of its existence, the manufactory made high-wheeled buggies but developed a national reputation in the 1890s for innovative racing sulkies. Toomey had several patents for his innovations in constructing lighter, faster sulkies. His greatest invention, the truss axle, revolutionized the sport of harness racing. The business continued under Toomey's careful guidance until his death in 1910. After that, his sons continued in the carriage business until 1915, when they contracted with Dodge and began selling automobiles.

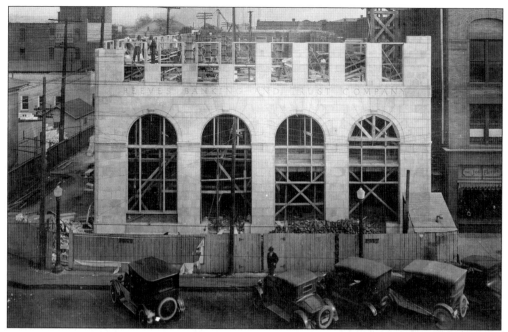

In 1903, Jeremiah E. Reeves established the Reeves Banking and Trust Company at 231 Factory Street (Tuscarawas Avenue). Later, in 1922, a new building was constructed at 232 West Third Street. Pictured is the construction of the new bank. Over the years, the bank expanded, and branches were opened in New Philadelphia, Sugarcreek, and Newcomerstown.

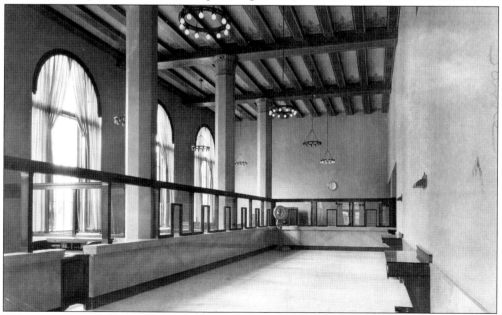

When it opened, the bank required a minimum deposit of only $1 to open an account, catering to the workingmen that Reeves employed. Many other businesses also operated in the Reeves bank building, including a billiard hall and a clothing and furniture store. The building remained in family hands until 1982. Today the building houses the Dover branch of Huntington Bank and the office of the Reeves Foundation.

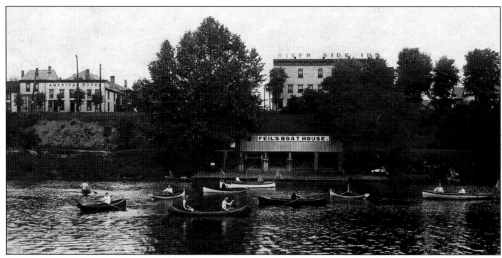

Shown is a view of the Tuscarawas River looking north between the Tuscarawas Avenue bridge and the Wooster Avenue bridge. On the banks of the river is Feil's boathouse. Above Feil's boathouse are the Riverside Hotel (right) and the American House Hotel.

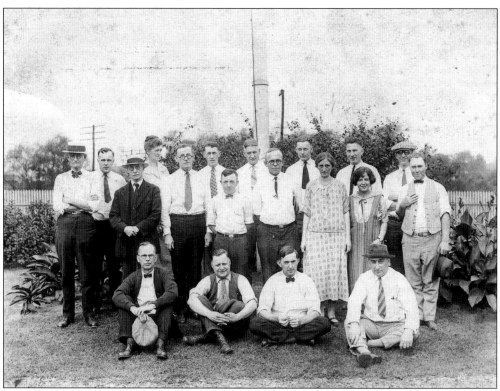

Pictured are the office employees of the American Sheet and Tin plate Company around 1920. From left to right are (first row) Fred Haas, William Uhl, Foster Flora, and William Vorherr; (second row) David Graham, John Jones, Jacob Hauk, Ralph Smith, J. Guy Ford, Edna Bailey, Bertha Pfeiffer Geiser, and Charles Walter; (third row) Forrest Gatchell, Nora Renkert, William Davis, W. H. Ashbaugh, Adolph Kneubuehl, Claude Herzig, and Carl Krantz.

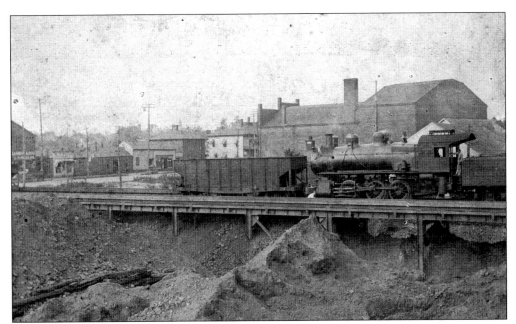

The Big Four Opera House (pictured top right) at 316–320 West Third Street opened on January 2, 1892, receiving its name after the four men who founded it: Jacob Horn, Joseph Beiter, Philip Schaefer, and Christian Deis. In 1904, the Hardesty brothers purchased the theater, renaming it the Hardesty Theater. Many well-known artists performed there, including Douglas Fairbanks, Will Rogers, minstrel performer Al Jolson, and the Sousa Band.

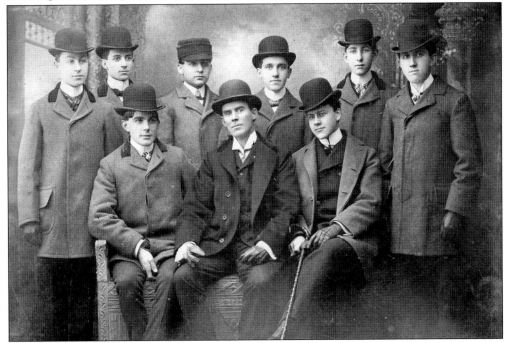

Pictured are the ushers for the Big Four Opera House in 1899, at the height of its popularity. From left to right are (first row) Joe Jenkins, William Cox, and Art Burchfield; (second row) William Wise, Arch Scheu, Ralph Toomey, Fred Fisher, Herbert Slingluff, and Homer Stalling.

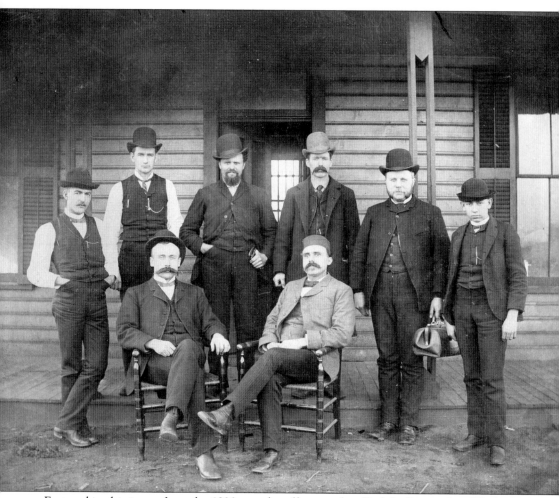

Featured in this image from the 1890s are the officers and staff of the Reeves Iron Works. From left to right are (first row) P. S. Cooper and Jeremiah E. Reeves; (second row) Thomas Haley, T. McCullough, Jabez Reeves, Thomas Richards, Alex Fraser, and Charles Landis. The Reeves Iron Works operated from 1883 through 1900 under the guidance of the Reeves family. It was located between Wooster Avenue and Tuscarawas Avenue just south of the Tuscarawas River. General Electric is currently located on this site.

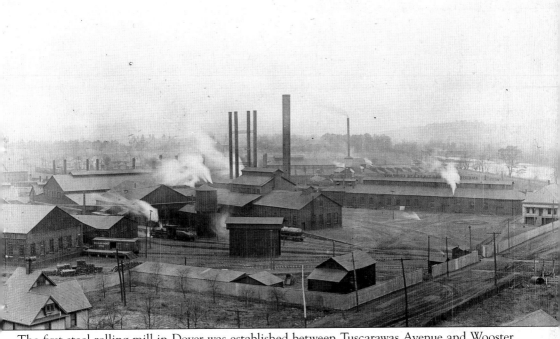

The first steel rolling mill in Dover was established between Tuscarawas Avenue and Wooster Avenue on the south bank of the Tuscarawas River in 1866 and 1867. The mill suffered a shaky existence until it was purchased by industrialist Jeremiah E. Reeves in 1883. Under his guidance, the Reeves Iron Works flourished, growing to employ over 850 men. In 1899, the mill was broken into two parts and sold to the American Sheet and Tin Plate Company, a subsidiary of the United States Steel Corporation. Although the tin mill was closed in 1901 after labor problems, the steel rolling mills were the backbone of northern Tuscarawas County industry for many years. In 1931, the Great Depression and changing economic conditions resulted in the closing of the American Sheet and Tin Plate Company.

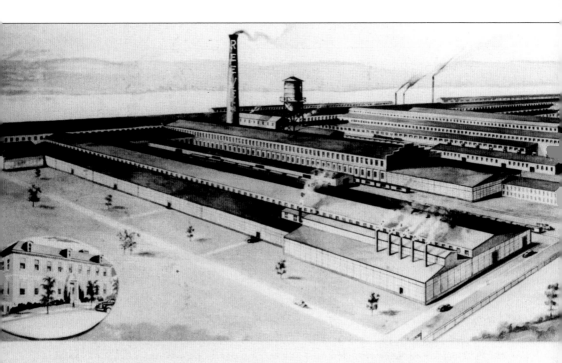

REEVES STEEL AND MFG. COMPANY
DOVER, OHIO.

In 1900, Samuel Jeremiah Reeves Sr. and his business partner Arthur J. Krantz established the Reeves Manufacturing Company. The company originally produced charcoal iron skelp or raw iron but became better known in later years for its production of galvanized steel products. In 1912, a galvanizing and sheet metal department was added to the mill, and it began to grow exponentially. By 1914, the mill was the largest independent company in Tuscarawas County, employing 600 men. In 1924, the company began producing products such as trash cans, coal hods, gas cans, buckets, and tubs. The mill reached its high-water mark in the 1940s when, during the war effort, the mill grew to employ over 1,500 men. Beginning in the late 1940s, a string of mergers lessened the Reeves family's control, and by 1957, it passed out of family hands entirely. The next 40 years brought a variety of name changes, mergers, and owners before the mill shut down permanently in 1999. For nearly a century, the Reeves Manufacturing Company served as the backbone of industry in Tuscarawas County.

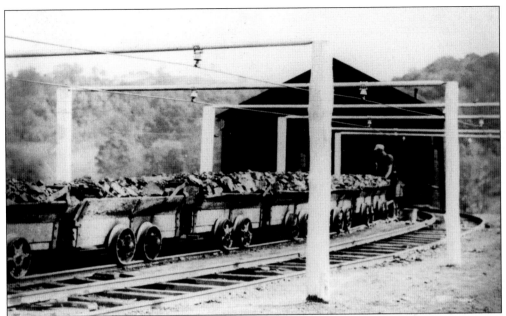

Located in Fairfield Township, the New England mines were founded by Dover industrialist Jeremiah E. Reeves. Around the mine, a flourishing small community of approximately 100 people developed, complete with its own school. The first residents of the small community were Welsh immigrants brought in by Reeves for their expertise in deep-shaft mining. After the decline of the mine in 1937, the small village slowly disappeared.

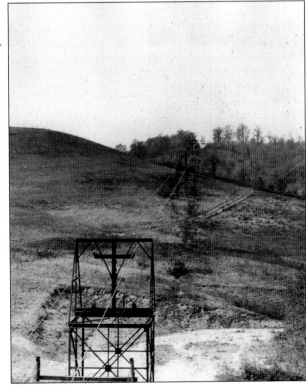

Once connected to the Reeves mines and the small community of New England, the aerial tramway delivered coal to the Reeves Manufacturing Company. The tramway consisted of 62 buckets that could move 300 tons of coal in an eight-hour day. As a safety precaution, the lowest point of the tramway was the Tuscarawas River. Therefore, if any malfunction took place, the bucket would fall harmlessly into the river.

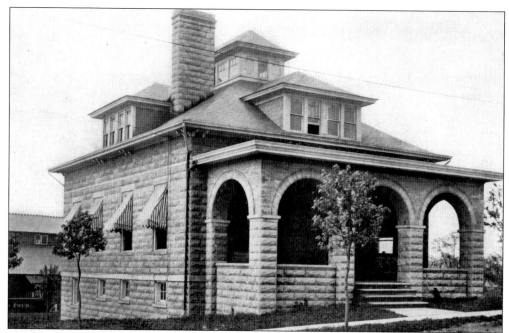

Shown are the original offices of the Reeves Manufacturing Company, located at 137 East Iron Avenue. The original Reeves office building was later added on to and expanded. Today the building still bears the name Reeves above its front entrance and houses the Dover offices of the 415 Group, Contini Financial, and Congressman Zack Space.

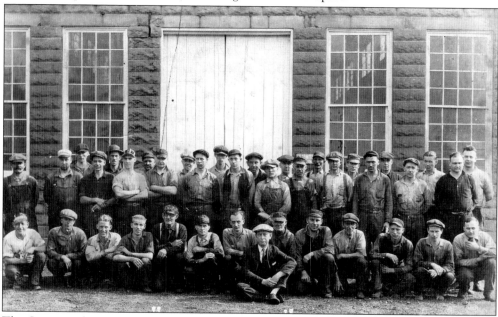

The Greer Steel Corporation was founded in 1917 by Agnes Reeves Greer and Herbert Chester Greer. Shown are the employees of the company, which produced cold rolled steel and was located just behind the Reeves Manufacturing Company. Today Greer Industries remains a strong company with interests in limestone, lime, asphalt, coal, newspapers, radio, caverns, golf courses, and steel.

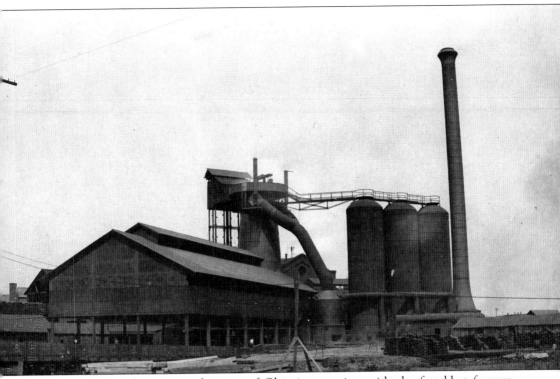

The history of blast furnaces in the state of Ohio is extensive, with the first blast furnace established in Mahoning County in 1808. Here in Dover, the first blast furnace was built in 1855. The Dover furnace changed hands many times, playing a role in the founding of many industries, including steel mills, foundries, and firebrick industries. In 1864, the furnace was purchased by the Dover Coal and Iron Company, with Samuel Croxton as the general manager. Under Croxton's guidance, the original furnace was rebuilt in 1878, with the earlier stone furnace being replaced by one made largely of plate iron. A double-track trestle was also constructed, and new tracks were laid to connect with the railroad. In 1881, the Penn Iron and Coal Company purchased the furnace and continued to operate it until 1905, when it was purchased by the Hanna Furnace Company. The furnace was again rebuilt and remained in operation through 1927 at the base of West Third Street in Dover.

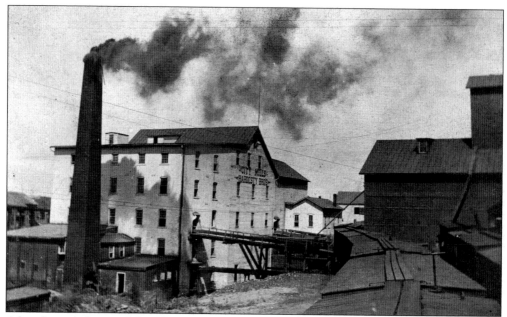

After the completion of the Ohio and Erie Canal in 1831, wheat prices rose dramatically. With the rising prices came a flourishing flour mill industry. The Dover City Mill was established by Nathaniel Hayden and Elijah Welty in 1842. The building sat on a millrace known as the Calico Ditch that ran from the Sugar Creek to the Ohio and Erie Canal. In 1866, the Hardesty brothers purchased the Dover mill.

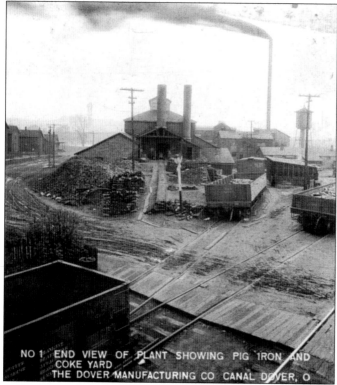

NO 1 END VIEW OF PLANT SHOWING PIG IRON AND COKE YARD
THE DOVER MANUFACTURING CO CANAL DOVER, O

The Dover Manufacturing Company was founded in 1899 by Charles Johnson. In 1900, it began the work of producing flatirons and sadirons with 40 employees. By 1908, the company had grown to employ 250 and shipped its products throughout the United States and to Europe and Australia. Pictured is the pig iron and coke yard with the factory in the background. The Dover Manufacturing Company was located at 524 River Street.

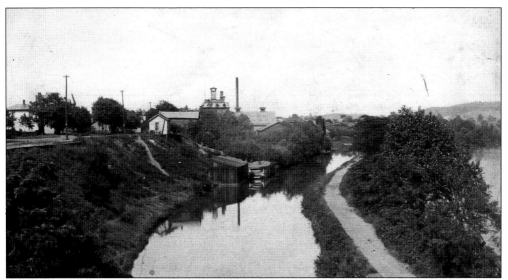

Heading northeast along the towpath, the smokestack of the Dover Brewing Company looms in the distance. The brewery was established as the Bernhard Brothers Brewery in 1872. In 1890, it was rebuilt with a new brew house, cold storage department, and a 20-ton ice-making machine. Fred Bernhard operated the brewery through 1899 when he retired, and the Dover Brewing Company took over, with Bernhard's son Christian as brewmaster.

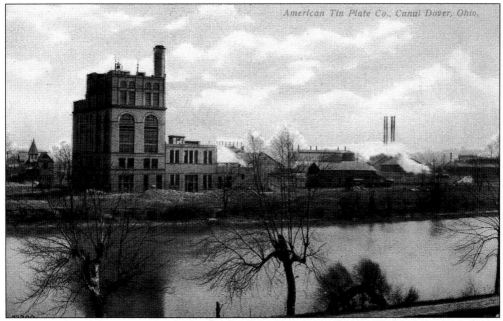

In 1903, work began on the Tuscarawas Valley Brewing Company. The total cost for its construction was $135,000, and it was paid for partially with locally owned stocks. The capacity of the brewery was 50,000 barrels annually. It was located on the corner of Wooster Avenue and Broadway at the present-day site of Chuck Nicholson Pontiac.

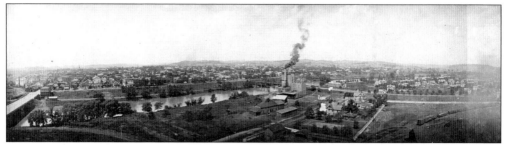

Pictured is a panoramic view of Dover around 1910. The Tuscarawas Valley Brewing Company is in the center. Also visible is the Dover riverfront, the tollhouse of the Ohio and Erie Canal, and the Dover Reading Rooms, the first library. On the far left is Dover's newly completed Tuscarawas Avenue bridge.

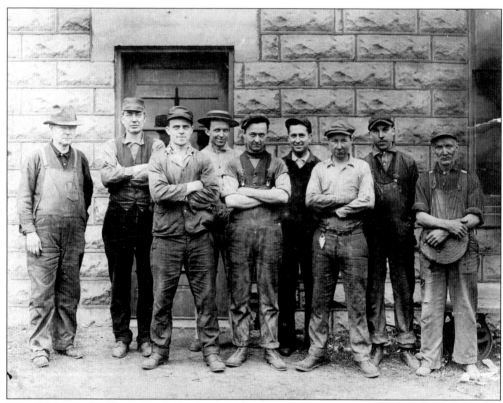

Founded around 1910, the Invincible Vacuum Cleaner Company was located at the foot of West Fifteenth Street. The company produced industrial vacuum equipment and heavy-duty portable vacuums for use in public spaces. It remained in business for over 60 years until it closed its doors in the late 1970s. Pictured is a group of Invincible Vacuum employees around 1930.

Five

THE CIVIL WAR
TO WORLD WAR I

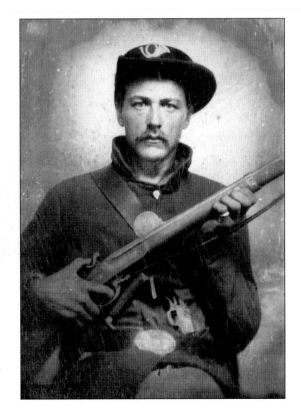

Milton Blickensderfer was born
on May 20, 1835, in Lancaster,
Pennsylvania, and moved to Tuscarawas
County as a small boy. In 1862, at the
age of 27, with three children at home,
Blickensderfer enlisted in the Union
army and was mustered into Company E
of the 126th Ohio Volunteer Infantry.
The 126th participated in over two
dozen battles and skirmishes, including
the battle of the Wilderness and those
at Spotsylvania Courthouse, Cold
Harbor, Petersburg, and Richmond. On
April 3, 1865, Blickensderfer stepped
into the annals of American history
at the siege of Petersburg. Surviving a
fierce charge and brutal hand-to-hand
combat, Blickensderfer captured a
Confederate battle flag. On May 3, 1865,
he was awarded the Medal of Honor for
his bravery.

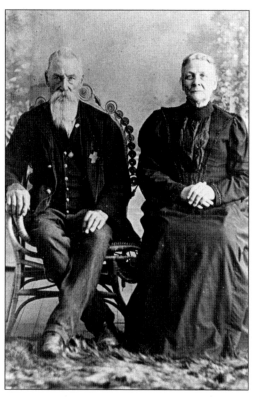

Milton and Mary Blickensderfer are pictured here. Milton is wearing his Medal of Honor. At the end of the 19th century, regimental reunions were popular and many soldiers wrote memoirs celebrating their service during the Civil War. Service in the Civil War was a badge of courage and a watershed moment for the generation who experienced it.

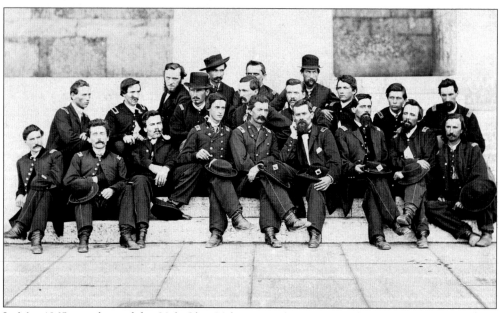

In May 1865, members of the 80th Ohio Volunteer Infantry traveled to Washington, D.C. The infantry unit was organized at Camp Meigs (Tuscarawas County Fairgrounds) between October 1861 and January 1862. Its many battles and skirmishes include those at Corinth and Vicksburg in Mississippi, Mission Ridge in Tennessee, and Gen. William T. Sherman's March to the Sea. The officers are pictured here.

Benjamin F. Croxton served as part of the 51st Ohio Volunteer Infantry. On November 22, 1864, he was promoted to captain of Company A, 51st Ohio Volunteer Infantry. He was mustered out with the rest of his unit in November 1865. Croxton was one of four brothers, two of whom served as officers in the same infantry.

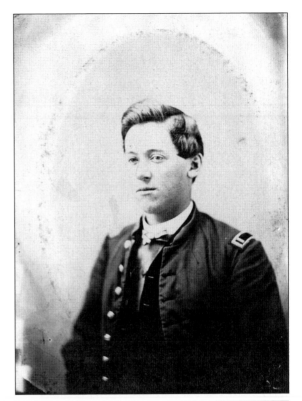

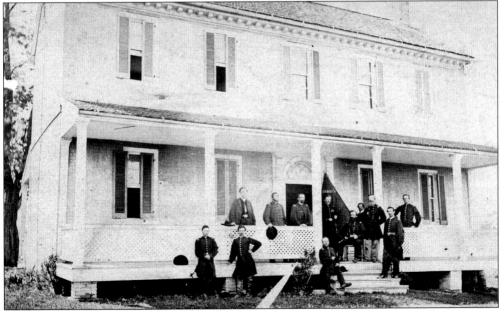

In the spring of 1865, officers of the 51st Ohio Volunteer Infantry were stationed at a home outside Nashville, Tennessee. Pictured to the left is Benjamin Croxton. The infantry was organized at Camp Meigs (Tuscarawas County Fairgrounds) on October 3, 1861, and saw action at Perryville, Kentucky; Stone River, Tennessee; Chickamauga, Georgia; Lookout Mountain in Georgia; and Mission Ridge in Tennessee.

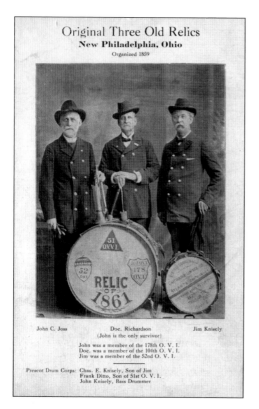

Original Three Old Relics
New Philadelphia, Ohio
Organized 1859

John C. Joss   Doc. Richardson   Jim Knisely
(John is the only survivor)

John was a member of the 178th O. V. I.
Doc. was a member of the 104th O. V. I.
Jim was a member of the 52nd O. V. I.

Present Drum Corps: Chas. E. Knisely, Son of Jim
Frank Ditto, Son of 51st O. V. I.
John Knisely, Bass Drummer

Pictured from left to right are John Joss, a veteran of the 178th Ohio Volunteer Infantry; Doc Richardson, a member of the 104th Ohio Volunteer Infantry; and Jim Knisely, a member of the 52nd Ohio Volunteer Infantry. In front of the men are three relics from the Civil War. The bugle that belonged to Joss is part of the permanent collection of the Dover Historical Society. It was used for taps.

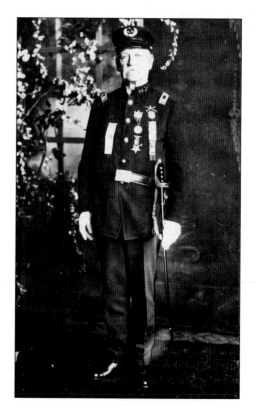

Dr. H. J. Peters was born in Pittsburgh, Pennsylvania, in 1842. In 1862, he mustered into the Union army at Fort Meigs (Tuscarawas County Fairgrounds) in Dover. During his service, Peters was taken prisoner at the Battle of Locust Grove, Virginia, on November 27, 1863. He spent two years in Confederate prisons, including such infamous places as Bell Island and Andersonville. He was released on February 27, 1865.

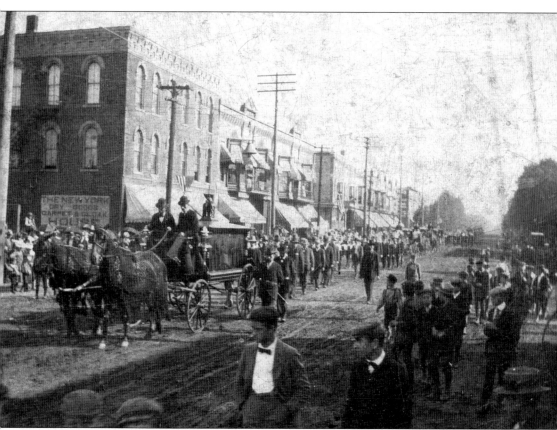

Tuscarawas County sent several hundred volunteers to battle during the Spanish-American War. It began on April 25, 1898, after the February sinking of the battleship the U.S.S. *Maine*, and ended less than four months later. During the summer of 1898, many patriotic parades, speeches, and celebrations were held in Dover on or around Independence Day.

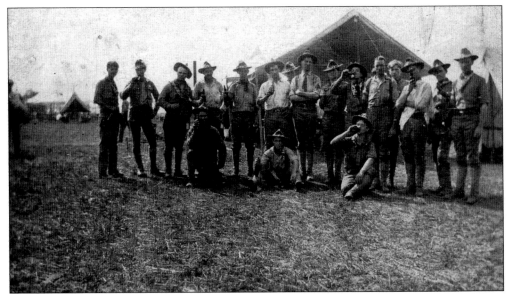

On August 13–20, 1906, 6,000 troops gathered as part of a militia muster of the Ohio National Guard. The encampment featured cavalry, infantry, and artillery and utilized 15,000 acres of the hilly countryside in northern Tuscarawas County. Dover men formed Company L of the Ohio National Guard and participated in all the activities. The highlight of the week was a military parade attended by Ohio's Gov. Andrew L. Harris.

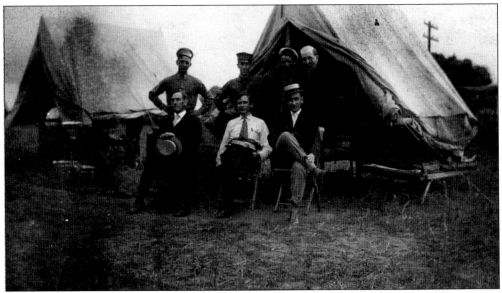

During the militia muster of the Ohio National Guard in 1906, troops from throughout the state were separated into two units. The blue unit was stationed at Strasburg, and the brown unit camped at Bolivar. On Saturday August 18, a mock battle was staged in the hills between the two camps. Civilians from the surrounding communities turned out in droves to watch it.

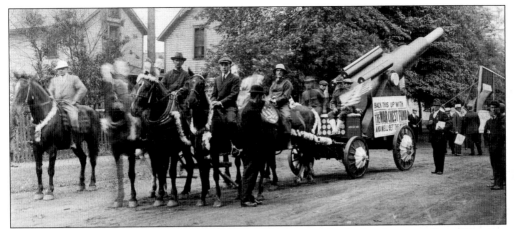

Many parades were held during World War I to help raise funds for the war effort. The sign underneath the cannon proclaims, "Back this up with the War Chest fund and we'll get the Kaiser." After the outbreak of war, the country quickly rallied around the troops through home front efforts. Americans were encouraged to conserve food, plant home gardens, save fuel, and buy war savings stamps.

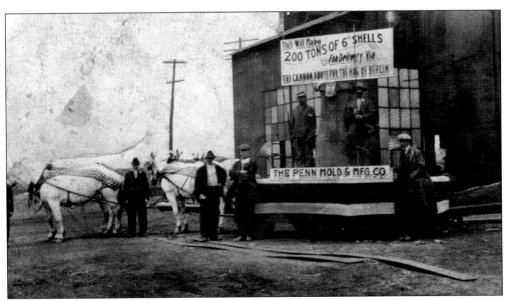

These men are shown preparing for a liberty bond parade in 1918. The Penn Mold Company was established in 1916 and received a government contract to produce shells during World War I. Their entry in the parade boasts, "This will make 200 tons of 6" Shells for delivery via the cannon route for the hog of Berlin."

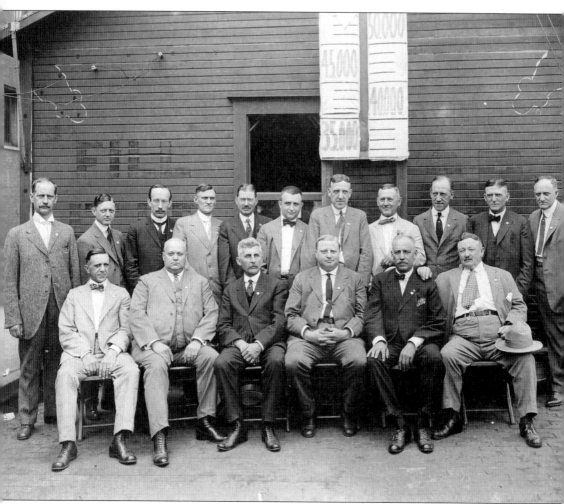

The directors of the Dover War Chest fund drive are pictured in front of the office and thermometer on Factory Street (Tuscarawas Avenue) in Dover. From left to right are (first row) G. A. Weinig, R. H. Nussdorfer, J. C Miller, A. H Reeves, H. W. Streb, and George Fertig; (second row) E. C. Seikel, H. D. Defenbacher, R. H. Brennecke, E. A. Schafer, L. O. Haug, M. C. Toomey, A. J. Krantz, S. J. Brister, J. A. Krantz, T. J. Haley, and C. S. Holland.

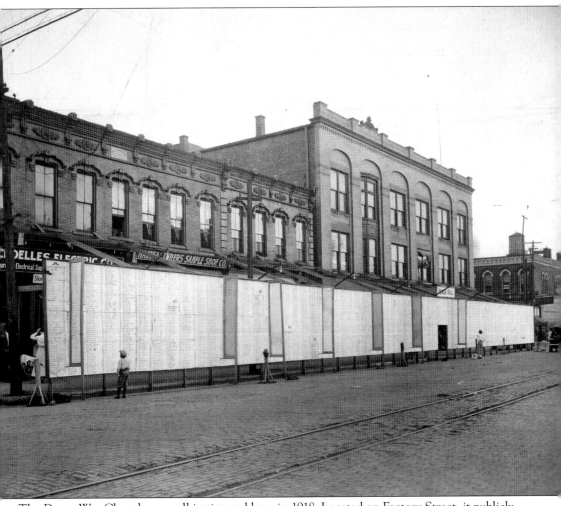

The Dover War Chest honor roll is pictured here in 1918. Located on Factory Street, it publicly recognized all those who contributed toward the fund-raising efforts and undoubtedly pressured those who had not contributed. In the background, Senhauser's clothing store is located on the far right.

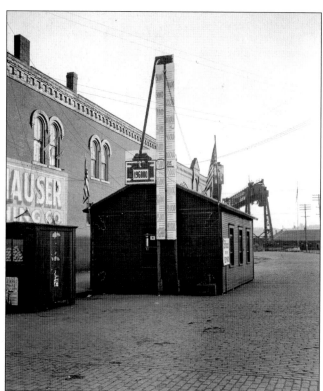

In April 1917, the United States entered World War I after attacks on seven American merchant ships. As the war progressed, efforts were made locally to support the troops. One example of this was the Dover War Chest fund drive. This thermometer was built on the corner of Factory and West Third Streets. Although the goal of the fund-raising campaign was $75,000, over $200,000 was collected.

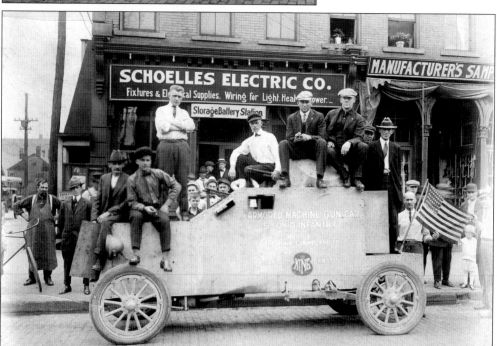

This armored machine gun car belonged to the 5th Ohio Infantry during World War I. It is pictured in front of Schoelles Electric Company at 211 East Fourth Street in Dover. Schoelles Electric Company did contracting work and sold electrical supplies.

Marching in a parade during World War I, the Boy Scouts of America played a very active role in helping to raise funds for the war effort. The organization was founded in the United States in 1910 and during the war adopted the slogan "Every Scout to Save a Soldier." In all, sale of liberty bonds during World War I raised $21.5 billion.

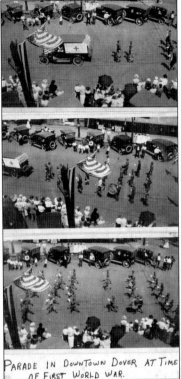

PARADE IN DOWNTOWN DOVER AT TIME OF FIRST WORLD WAR.

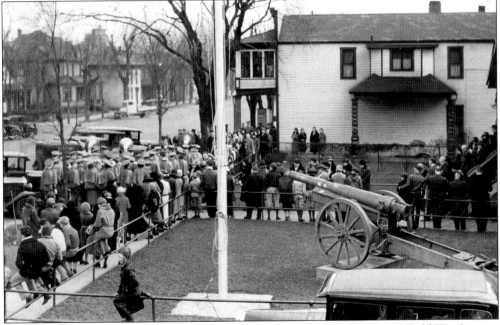

Pictured is a band gathering in front of Memorial Hall in the 1920s. During World War I, many drives, fund-raisers, and benefits were held to boost the war effort. At the conclusion of the war, any unused funds were turned over to the American Legion to build Memorial Hall. Memorial Hall is located at 410 North Wooster Avenue.

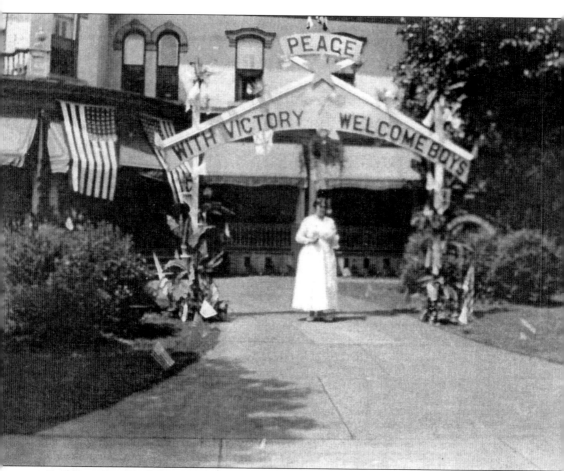

On November 11, 1918, at 2:45 a.m., word reached Dover that an armistice had been signed, effectively ending World War I. The following day, celebrations broke out throughout Tuscarawas County, with impromptu parades in both Dover and New Philadelphia. Later November 11 was declared a national holiday, first as Armistice Day and after World War II as Veterans Day. Pictured is the Reeves home on East Iron Avenue, decorated to welcome home the troops.

Six

DOVER CITY AND SOCIAL SERVICES

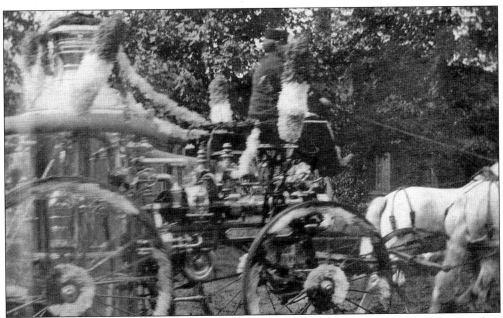

In 1873, the Dover Fire Department was formed, and Samuel J. Toomey, a local carriage maker, was named the first fire chief. Initially the department used a secondhand steam engine purchased in Allegheny, Pennsylvania. In 1873, when a serious fire threatened the lower end of Tuscarawas Avenue (Factory Street), "Old Ironsides," as the pump was nicknamed, performed well. However, after the fire was under control, the boiler exploded on the original pumper. In 1874, the city authorized the department to purchase a rotary gear pumper from the Silsby Company of Seneca Falls, New York. Pictured above is the 1874 Silsby steam pumper decorated for a 1903 parade.

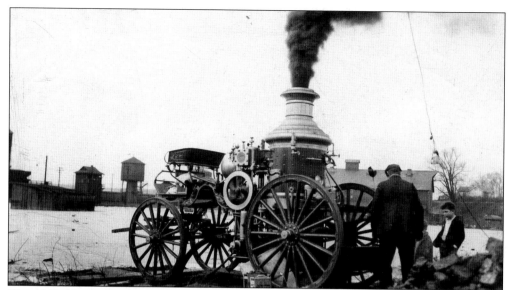

The 1907 Ahrens-Fox pumper was purchased by the Dover Fire Department for $6,800 as a replacement for the 1873 Silsby steamer. The pumper was a horseless steam fire engine and remained part of the department for 30 years. Last used to help control floodwaters in 1937, it was retired and sold to the Western Mutual Insurance Company in Columbus. Today the pumper is at the Ohio Historical Society.

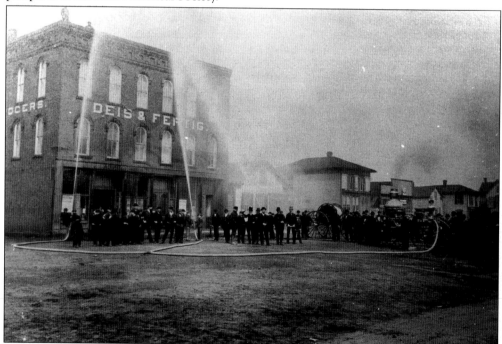

On March 19, 1886, the Dover Fire Department publicly displayed its new Silsby rotary pumper. The building pictured is the Deis-Fertig Wholesale grocery located on the northeast corner of Third Street and Tuscarawas Avenue. The water for the demonstration was taken from underground cisterns that were once commonplace in Dover. The Silsby rotary pumper propelled water easily over the three-story building.

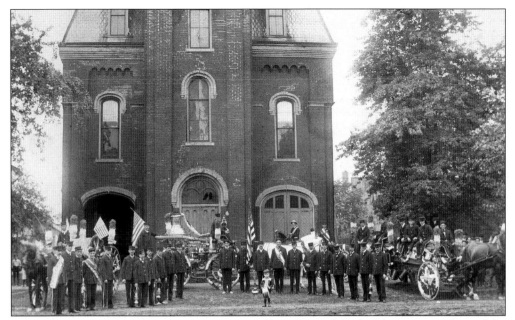

Pictured around 1901 is the 1871 Dover City Hall. In front of the building are members of the fire department dressed in formal attire for a parade. This version of city hall is the predecessor of the present-day municipal building. It was razed when the current city hall was constructed. The building was on the corner of Wooster Avenue and Third Street, but closer to Wooster Avenue than the current building.

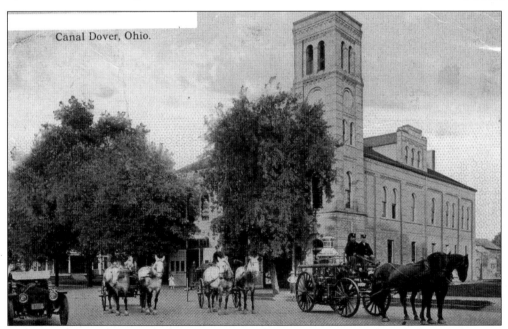

Canal Dover, Ohio.

This postcard features members of the city's fire department in front of city hall, with the 1907 Ahrens-Fox pumper front and center. In 1874, a large bell was installed at city hall to notify the volunteer firefighters of a blaze. In 1901, when the city built a replacement for the 1871 structure, the fire bell was transferred to the new tower.

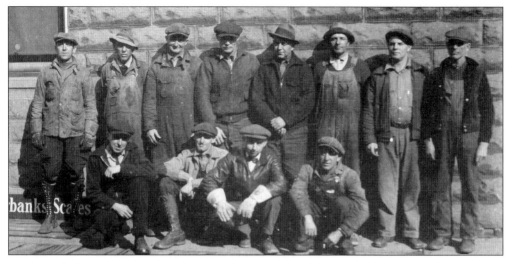

The employees of the City of Dover Electric Department are shown around 1936. Third from the left (kneeling) is Supt. A. B. Klyne. Klyne served as Dover's chief electrician for 41 years. At the time he assumed the position of chief electrician, Dover had only 500 homes with electrical service and one traffic light. (Courtesy of the City of Dover Electric Department.)

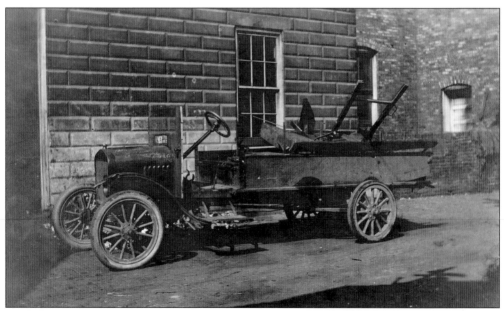

Pictured is a City of Dover Electric Department truck around 1920. (Courtesy of the City of Dover Electric Department.)

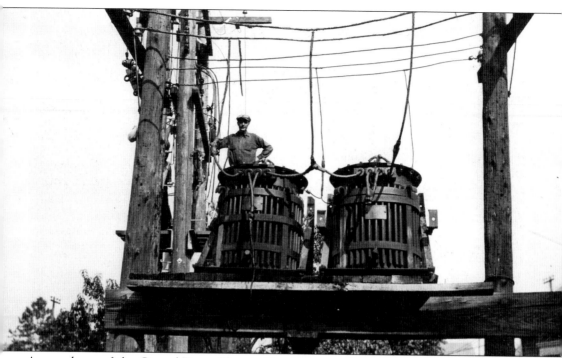

An employee of the City of Dover Electric Department is shown working on a transformer around 1932. Although Dover approved a bond issue to build a municipal electric light plant in 1898, the city's dream of producing its own power did not become a reality until February 15, 1910. The reason for the delay was the difficult time the city faced in selling bonds for the new light plant along with pending litigation filed by an independent electric company. Prior to 1909, the power for electric lights in downtown Dover was provided by the Tuscarawas County Light and Power Company. It contracted with the city to provide power and used litigation to stall the city's plans to construct its own power source. After a long battle, the contract between the City of Dover and the Tuscarawas County Light and Power Company expired on December 1, 1909, and the downtown lights went out. The downtown remained dark until February 15, 1910, when the municipal light plant was finished. (Courtesy of the City of Dover Electric Department.)

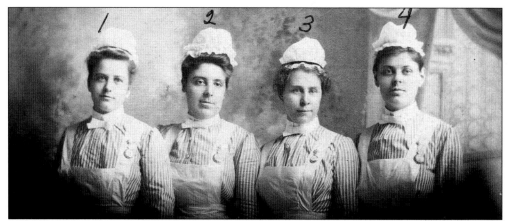

On March 16, 1901, the Tuscarawas County Hospital Association was organized. Without the funds to build a new hospital, a home on West Fourth Street was secured and outfitted with an operating room. The hospital could accommodate six patients and treated all diseases provided the patients were not considered contagious. Pictured from left to right are nurses Emma L. Schoelles, Minnie Linton, Edith G. Summers, and Emma Sehl around 1903.

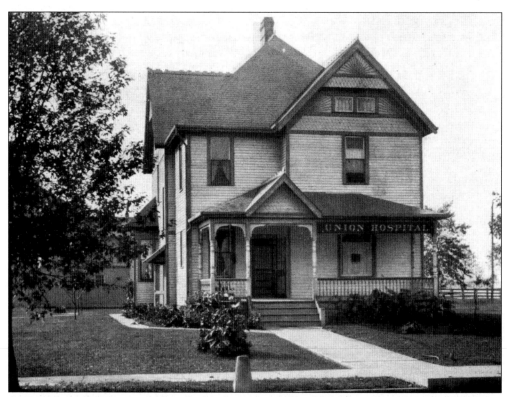

On March 15, 1906, a temporary hospital was established in a leased home at 506 East Iron Avenue. The location was chosen for the purity and quality of the wells and for its central location between Dover and New Philadelphia. The site was also conveniently located on the Northern Ohio Traction and Light Company streetcar line. This first Union Hospital accommodated up to 20 patients.

UNION DEPOT

BENEFIT OF UNION HOSPITAL

ADMIT ONE

HARDESTY THEATRE

SEPTEMBER 7, 1906   PRICE 25c

This ticket can be exchanged for a reserved seat at The Sykes Co., without additional cost.

On September 7, 1906, a benefit was held at the Hardesty Theater, the day after the cornerstone of the new hospital was laid. Another benefit featured a baseball game played at the Tuscarawas County Fairgrounds. The game was held on October 24, 1908, and featured many recognizable names, such as Denton True "Cy" Young and Honus Wagner. Young's team won 4-1, with 8,000 spectators watching.

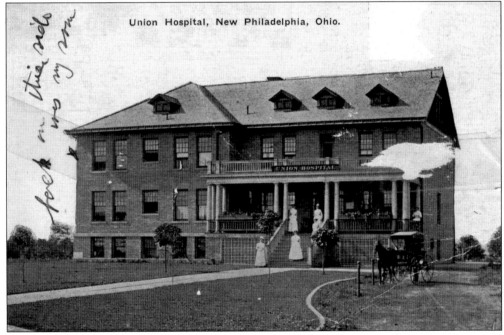

Union Hospital, New Philadelphia, Ohio.

When the new Union Hospital was completed and dedicated on March 19, 1909, it could accommodate 60 patients and featured its own kitchen, laundry, cleansing and sterilizing machines, and elevator. The total cost for construction of the hospital was $17,000, which was $7,000 over the budget.

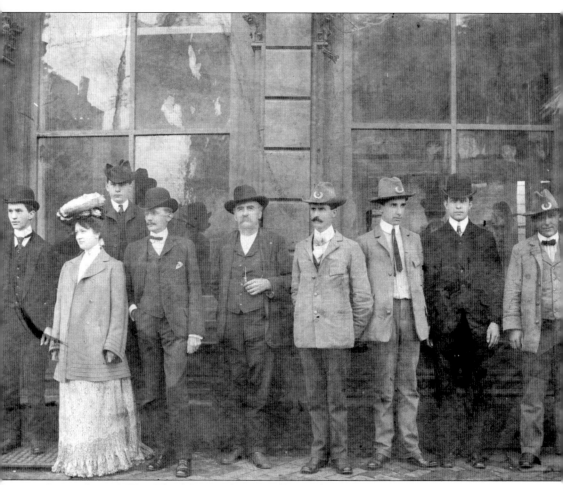

Located at 232 West Third Street, the post office in the early 19th century was on the lot where Huntington Bank sits today. Pictured is the staff of the post office around 1900. From left to right are Walter Weber, Carrie Huff, Walter B. Scott, W. G. Immel, W. W. Scott (postmaster), Perry Robert, Guy Lucas, Horace Dell, and Jim Barr.

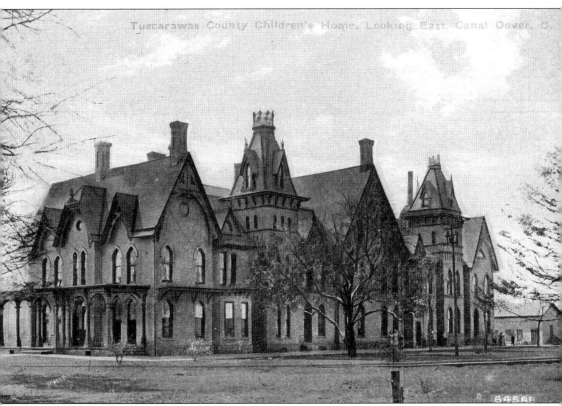

Tuscarawas County Children's Home, Looking East, Canal Dover, O.

Once located on Tuscarawas Avenue in Dover, the Tuscarawas County Children's Home opened in 1881. The home was originally the residence of Augustus Wilhelmi, a dealer in coal and iron ore. He sold the home to the county for $25,000 in 1881 for the purpose of establishing an orphanage. An addition to the home doubled its size, allowing it to accommodate more than 100 children in most years and nearly 150 during the Great Depression. The home was operated through 1956 when the Tuscarawas County Welfare Department opted to place children in foster homes and cease operation of the children's home.

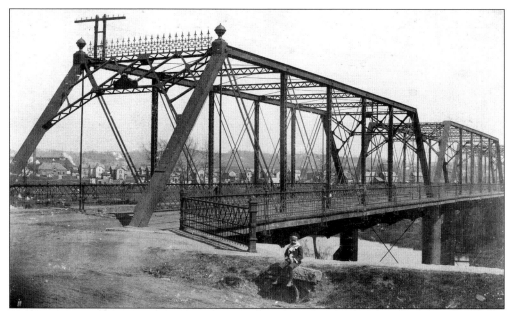

Pictured is Dover's first Wooster Avenue bridge built in 1893 by the Wrought Iron Bridge Company of Canton. When the final plank of the bridge was laid, there was a race to see who could be the first to cross the bridge in a carriage. The winners were H. H. Scheu and local newspaper editor W. W. Scott, who completed the crossing in Scheu's luxury buggy.

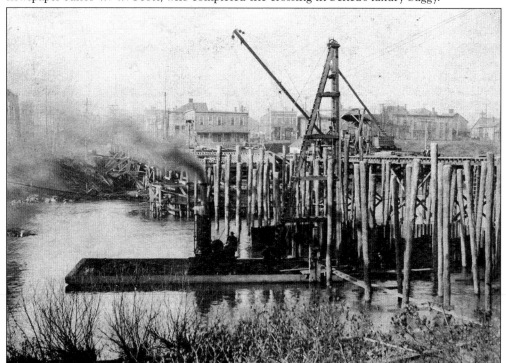

The current Tuscarawas Avenue bridge was constructed in 1906 at a cost of $110,000. At the base of the bridge sat the tollhouse for the Ohio and Erie Canal. Prior to the destruction of the canal during the flood of 1913, it passed underneath one of the of the bridge's four arches.

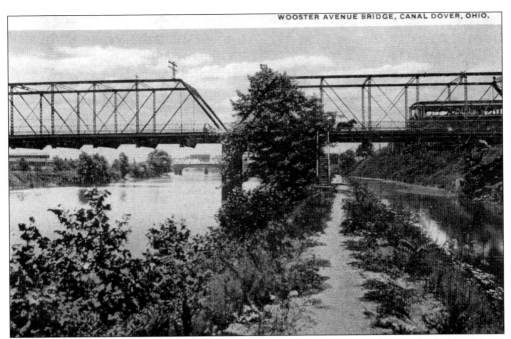

The old iron Wooster Avenue bridge was a fixture of Dover's riverfront for many years. This image, showing the area sometime between 1906 and 1913, includes multiple modes of transportation. In the background is the Tuscarawas Avenue bridge that was constructed in 1906.

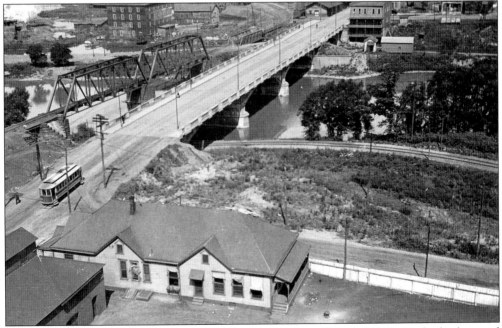

This view features the Tuscarawas Avenue bridge between 1906 and 1913. In the background is the tollhouse and the Dover Reading Rooms. The Dover Reading Rooms were located just opposite the tollhouse at 99 Factory Street. They were maintained as a library by the American Sheet and Tin Plate Company until 1907, when a brick residence across from Oak Grove School was dedicated as the first public library.

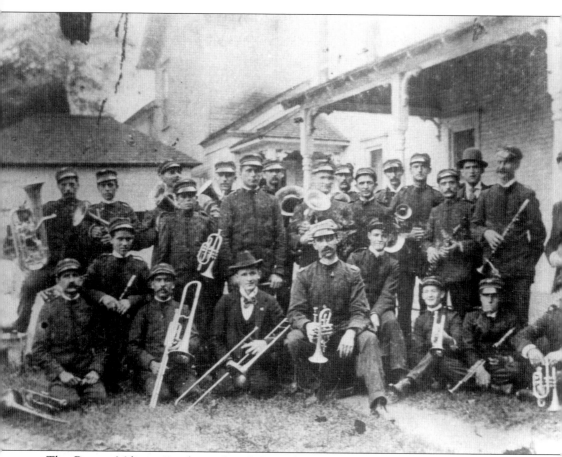

The Reeves Military Band was founded in the 1890s and supported financially by Dover industrialist Jeremiah E. Reeves. In an article from the *Iron Valley Reporter*, the band is described as dressing in military blue uniforms braided in black. Members also wore caps with the monogram "R.M.B." in gold. In addition to patriotic music, the band was known to play sacred or religious music during their Sunday concerts.

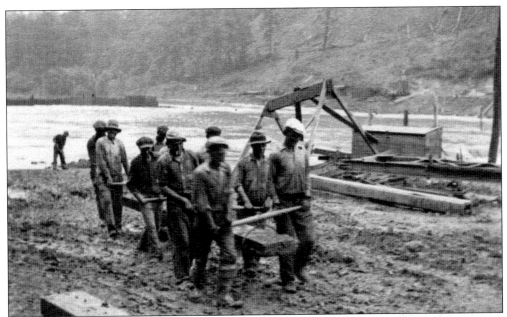

In 1936, work began on the construction of the Dover Dam. Created as part of Pres. Franklin D. Roosevelt's New Deal, the Muskingum Watershed Conservancy District grew to employ 5,178 people in 1936. Of that number, 1,053 worked on the Dover Dam. In September 1937, the last of the concrete was poured for the new dam, and a formal dedication of the conservancy district took place on July 17, 1938.

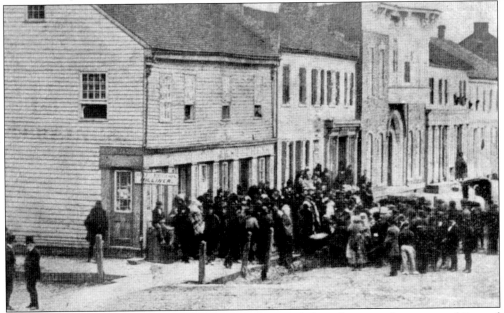

In 1873, a local temperance society, the Crusaders, raided a saloon on the corner of Second Street and Tuscarawas Avenue. The group purchased all the liquor in the saloon and proceeded to empty it into the gutter in front of the building. Beginning in the 1870s, temperance societies began to gain support. Just a year after the Dover raid, the national Woman's Christian Temperance Union was founded in Cleveland.

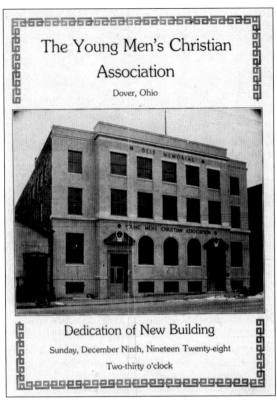

Dover's downtown YMCA was dedicated on December 9, 1928. Located at 307–311 Tuscarawas Avenue, the YMCA was housed in the Deis Memorial building. Prior to the dedication, the YMCA met above the Brucks Hardware Store on West Third Street. First formed on December 29, 1919, the YMCA continued to operate on Tuscarawas Avenue until the early 1970s, when it moved to its current location at 600 Monroe Street.

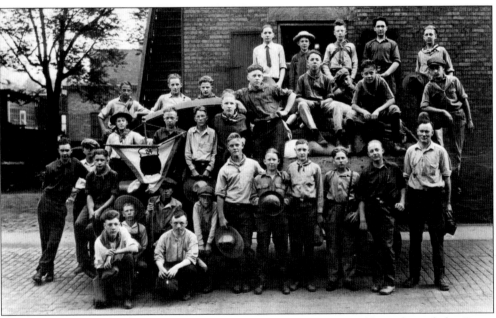

During the early days of the Tuscarawas County YMCA, a group of boys formed the Dover Gypsy Hikers. The group met to tackle hikes of up to 50 miles. This picture was taken in Cherry Alley before the group embarked on a trip to Camp Nelson Dodd on June 24, 1924. Any young man who could prove he had walked at least 35 miles was awarded a Gypsy Hiker emblem.

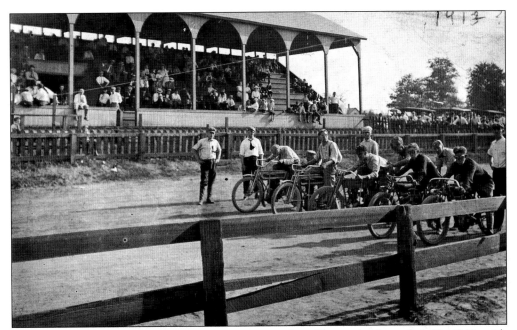

The Tuscarawas Agricultural Society was organized in Dover on November 10, 1849, with George Slingluff as the society's first president. By 1851, the society recognized the importance of establishing fairgrounds. The first county fair to take place on the present-day fairgrounds was held on October 14–15, 1852. Pictured above is a motorcycle race held at the fairgrounds track. The first track was constructed on the grounds in 1859.

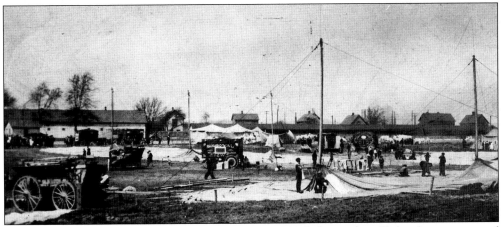

The Rhoda Royal Circus came to Dover on May 10, 1920. It featured an 80-foot big top tent and set up at the fairgrounds. During the early 20th century, circuses crisscrossed the United States, doing an especially good business in areas like Kentucky, West Virginia, and Ohio. The Rhoda Royal Circus was in business from 1919 to 1922.

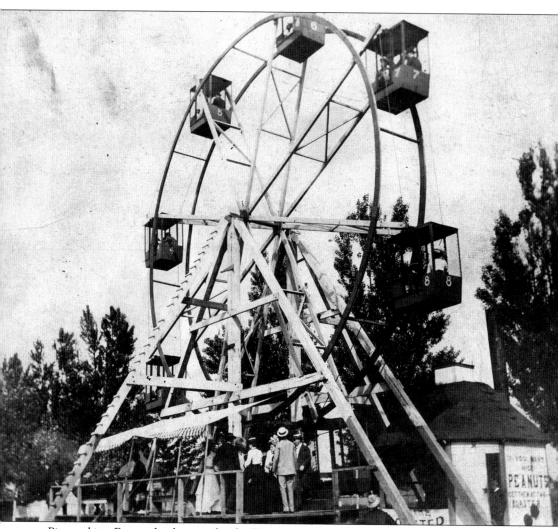

Pictured is a Ferris wheel set up for the Tuscarawas County Fair. The county hosted its first fair on October 15–16, 1850, on the property of Dover resident Henry Hayden. Hayden's Grove, as the property was known, was eventually acquired by Dover city schools and today is the site of the current Dover High School. Since 1850, Tuscarawas County has hosted an annual fair every year but 1861. In 1861, the fair was cancelled as the grounds were being used for Civil War training.

Seven

THE FLOOD OF 1913

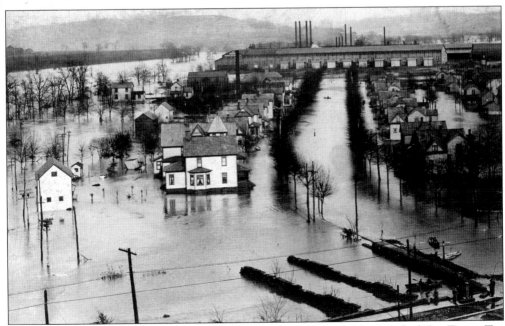

One of the hardest hit areas during the 1913 flood was the neighborhood of Tin Town. Tin Town was the brainchild of Dover industrialist Jeremiah E. Reeves, who built the homes for his workers. The neighborhood is located in a low-lying area of Dover on the banks of the Tuscarawas River.

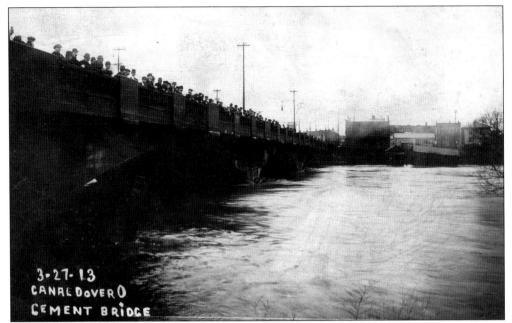

Residents of Dover gather on the Tuscarawas Avenue bridge to marvel at the floodwaters. Beginning on March 20, 1913, rains began to fall on the Tuscarawas River valley and did not stop for the next six days. Some estimates put the five-day rainfall total at nearly 12 inches.

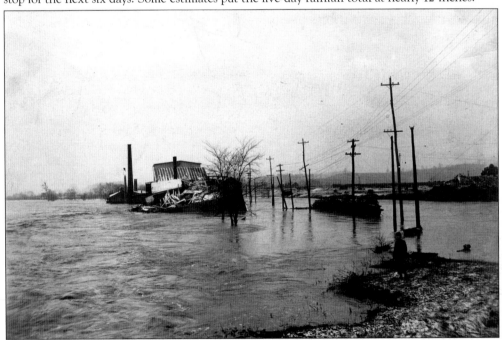

Pictured are what remained of the Dover Manufacturing Company and the Wagner Brothers foundry. The foundry was located between the canal and the Tuscarawas River and suffered extensive damage during the flood of 1913. After the flood, the brothers moved their business from the riverfront to the foot of West Fifteenth Street, where they produced sewer pipe dies and repaired engines, pumps, and other machinery.

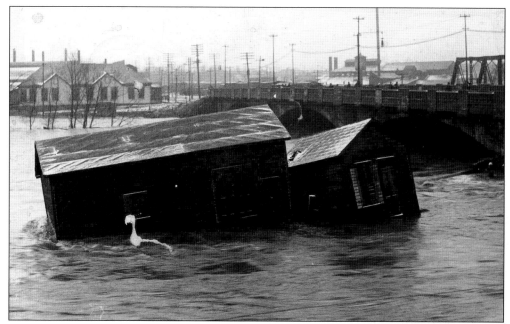

During the flood of 1913, Tuscarawas County's only canal tollhouse was swept away by the fierce currents of the river. The towpath was also a casualty of the floodwaters, as it was completely washed away west of the Tuscarawas Avenue bridge. On March 27, 1913, the river reached its height and crested at nearly three and a half feet higher than the previous flood record set in 1898.

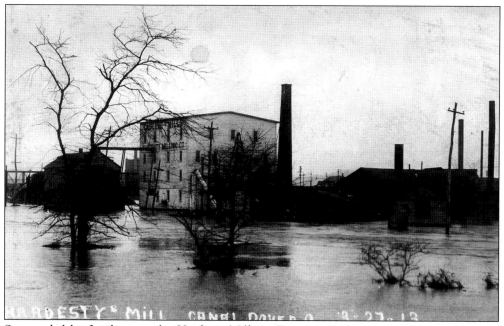

Surrounded by floodwaters, the Hardesty Milling Company is shown at the base of Second Street in Dover.

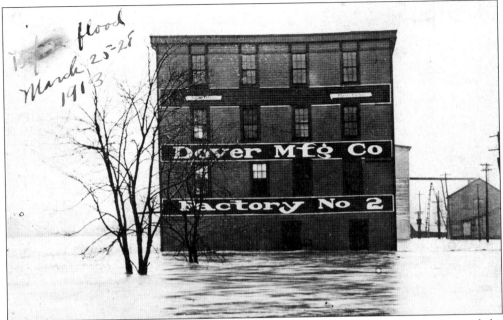

The Dover Manufacturing Company was located at 524 River Street. At the time of the flood, it was a well-known producer of asbestos sadirons. Both the factory and offices were located back behind what is today McMillan Heating and Cooling on the south side of the Tuscarawas River.

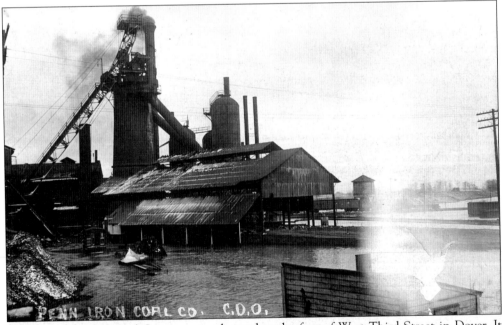

The Penn Iron and Coal Company was located at the foot of West Third Street in Dover. It manufactured pig iron used in the steelmaking process. The space originally housed Dover's blast furnace and was later operated as Shenango. Today the old Penn Iron and Coal Company is used as warehouse space.

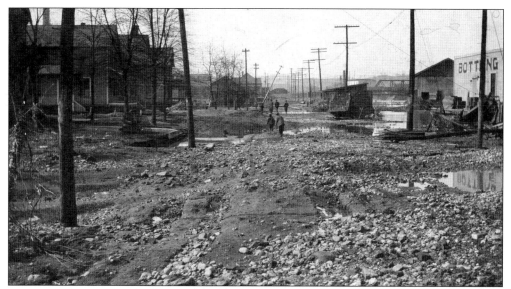

During the flood of 1913, Tin Town was submerged under raging floodwaters. One resident, John Mainwaring, recalls the water rising to nearly five feet above the first floor of his home. When his family was able to return home, they found themselves shoveling mud and debris out of their second-story windows. Many families, including Mainwaring's, moved away from Tin Town after the 1913 flood.

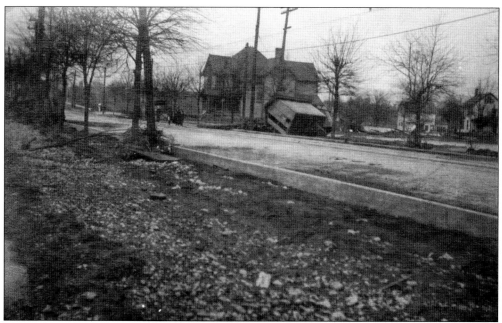

Many buildings along the Tuscarawas River suffered extensive damage during the flood of 1913. In addition to cleanup, a number of businesses had their foundations washed out, collapsing with loud crashes that were heard by the displaced residents at the Riverside Inn.

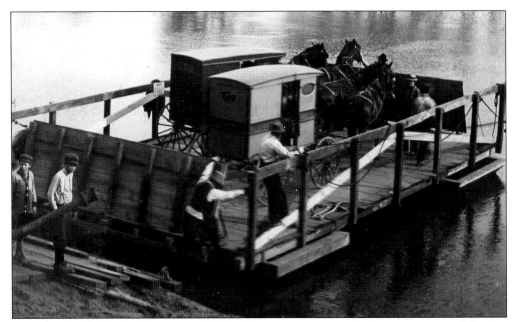

During the flood, many of the county's bridges were swept away, forcing a return to simpler times. Ferries were again put to use in transporting people and goods across the Tuscarawas River. In order to rebuild many of the bridges along the river, bond issues were raised, creating large debts that the county had to pay for many years to come.

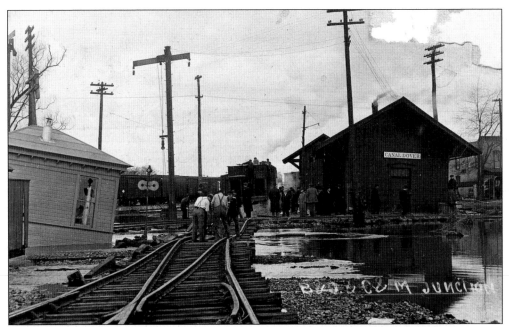

Ohio's railroads suffered devastating losses during the flood of 1913, with many miles of track washed away and bridges destroyed. In some cases, it took years before regular operation was restored. Sitting at the foot of West Third Street near Broad Street, the Baltimore and Ohio Railroad junction was heavily damaged during the flood of 1913. Pictured are the freight and passenger stations.

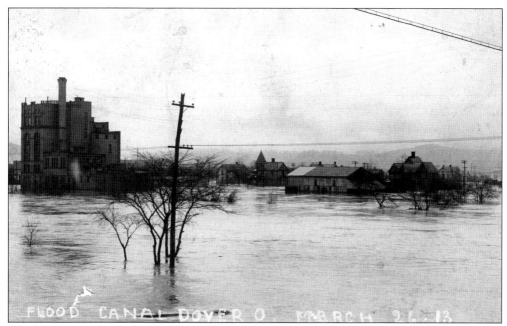

The Tuscarawas Valley Brewing Company was founded in 1903. In addition to beer, it also produced ice from distilled water. The brewery was located on the corner of Wooster Avenue and Broadway where Chuck Nicholson Pontiac is today. Sitting on the banks of the Tuscarawas River, the brewery sustained heavy damage during the 1913 flood.

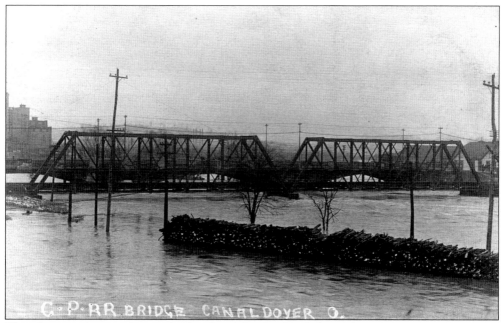

This photograph was taken at the height of the flood and shows the water at its highest level. The iron bridge in the foreground is the railroad bridge. Just behind the railroad bridge is the Tuscarawas Avenue bridge with the Tuscarawas Valley Brewing Company in the distance.

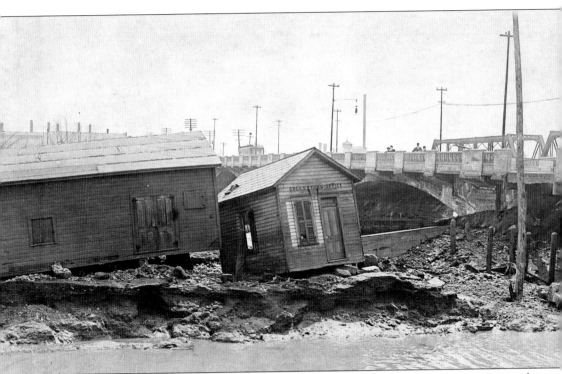

When the floodwaters finally receded, the damage to the riverfront was extensive. Pictured is the collector's office or tollhouse for the Ohio and Erie Canal. Also visible is an example of the damage to the canal. Silt from the river washed over its banks and coated everything in sight with thick mud and rocks. Faced with the cost of dredging and redigging portions of the canal, the state instead chose to discontinue much of its operation.

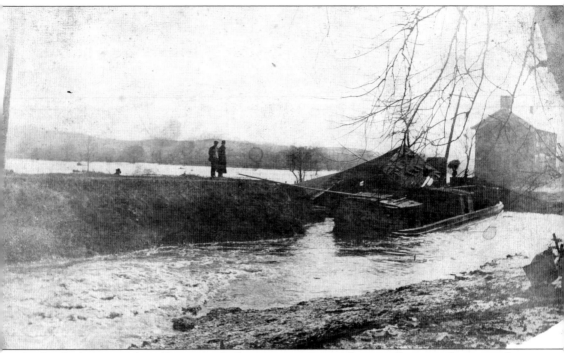

The flood of 1913 was literally a watershed moment in Dover's history, changing the city and the lives of many residents. The flood marked the end of the Ohio and Erie Canal, as the cost of rebuilding greatly outweighed the potential of the declining canal. The floodwaters were responsible for the loss of many public services, including all electric, water, telephones, and telegraph lines. Many areas of the city were evacuated as floodwaters rose, and refugees packed the rooms at the Riverside Inn. Even after the rains stopped, Dover faced a food shortage and had no available milk, as farmers were unable to get their product into the city. Pictured are the remains of a canal boat damaged during the flood.

www.arcadiapublishing.com

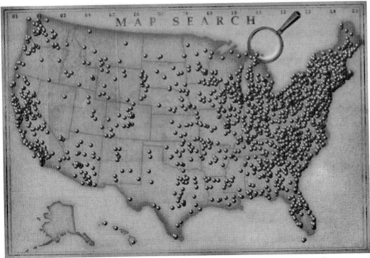

MAP SEARCH

Discover books about the town where you grew up, the cities where your friends and families live, the town where your parents met, or even that retirement spot you've been dreaming about. Our Web site provides history lovers with exclusive deals, advanced notification about new titles, e-mail alerts of author events, and much more.

MADE IN THE

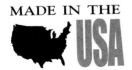

USA

Arcadia Publishing, the leading local history publisher in the United States, is committed to making history accessible and meaningful through publishing books that celebrate and preserve the heritage of America's people and places. Consistent with our mission to preserve history on a local level, this book was printed in South Carolina on American-made paper and manufactured entirely in the United States.

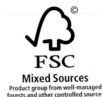
Find Your Place in History.